Cheers for
The Ultimate Pinewood Derby Experience

Barlow Packer's book is great read about the fun and real purpose behind the Pinewood Derby. It made me realize that all the work I do organizing Pinewood Derby events is really worth it.
   - *Douglas A., Cub Scout Pack Master*

My Dad helped me build my car for speed using most of the tips in Mr. Packer's book. We didn't lose one heat! We couldn't believe how much faster our new car was when we raced it against the one we built last year.
   - *Braydon, Cub Scout*

How fortunate I was to have first-hand experience with the tips and lessons shared in Barlow Packer's book. As a result, my son's car was a full length winner in each of the heats. It was a great evening and a great memory for me and my son. Most important, building my son's Pinewood Derby car together allowed us to connect and helped me further shape his life and progress. Truly a great way to connect kids and parents.
   - *Mitch S.*

The Ultimate Pinewood Derby Experience is a must read for those who want to know what they are really building for their next Pinewood Derby.
   - *Kim P., A Single Mom*

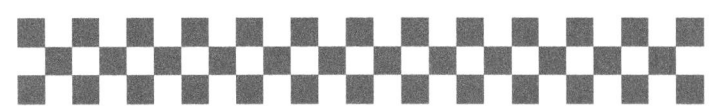

The Ultimate Pinewood Derby Experience

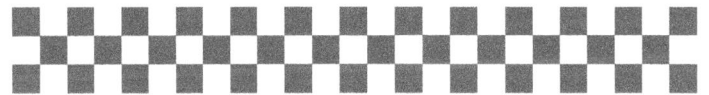

The Ultimate Pinewood Derby Experience

Making the Most of
Four Wheels,
Four Nails,
a Block of Wood,
and Your Kid

Plus: Ten Great Tips for
Building a Faster Car

By Dr. Barlow L. Packer

Surrogate Press™

Copyright ©2017 Barlow L. Packer

All rights reserved.

No part of this publication may be reproduced,
stored in a retrieval system, or transmitted in any form or by
any means, electronic, mechanical, photocopying, recording, or
otherwise, without written permission of the author.

Published in the United States by
Surrogate Press™
an imprint of Faceted Press

Surrogate Press, LLC

SurrogatePress.com

ISBN: 978-1-947459-06-9

Library of Congress Control Number: 2017958540

Book cover design by: Michelle Rayner, Cosmic Design

Interior design by: Katie Mullaly, Surrogate Press®

Dedicated to:

Curtis, Gardiner, McKay

Mitchell, Isaac, Tayden

Wyatt, Josh, Noah, and Eli

Table of Contents

Introduction: Something Great is About to Happen..........1

Lesson One: It Takes a Village 6

Lesson Two: The Value of Tradition.................................11

Lesson Three: The Importance of Creating a Goal...........17

Lesson Four: Enjoy the Learning 21

Lesson Five: The Importance of Planning,
Committing, and Working..26

Lesson Six: Learning That Patience Is a Virtue.................31

Lesson Seven: Fun is More Fun if You Have
Someone to Have It With..37

Lesson Eight: If Something is Worth Doing,
It's Worth Doing Well 44

Lesson Nine: Learning How to Determine
What is Fact or "Friction"...52

Lesson Ten: There are Two Kinds of Alignment...............61

Lesson Eleven: The Measure You Give Is
the Measure You Get Back...68

Lesson Twelve: Learning to Feel and
Express Gratitude 75

Conclusion: The Finish Line 83

Appendix A: Winning Car Tips 85

   Winning Car Tip # 1: Shape Your Car Block.............87

   Winning Car Tip #2: Prepare Your Wheels................88

   Wining Car Tip #3: Prepare Your Axle Holes 90

   Winning Car Tip #4: Prepare Your Axles...................92

   Winning Car Tip #5: Finishing your Car Body 94

   Winning Car Tip #6: Place the Weight
   in Your Car 94

   Winning Car Tip #7: Weigh and Assemble
   Your Car...96

   Winning Car Tip #8: Tune Your Car 97

   Winning Car Tip #9: Test Your Car On a
   Real Track If Possible...99

   Winning Car Tip #10: Race Your Car,
   Bring Home a Trophy 100

About the Author 101

Something Great is About to Happen

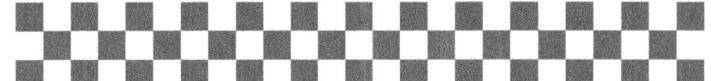

Introduction

You arrive home from work one day and as you walk into your house you see on the kitchen counter that very recognizable little box your son or daughter brought home from a Cub Scout meeting[1]. It's the Pinewood Derby Car Kit, containing four wheels, four nails, and a block of wood. You know immediately that it's Pinewood Derby time again.

A flood of memories (possibly from your own Pinewood Derby days) makes you realize the time commitment required to work with your child as you help him or her prepare (maybe for the first time) for a Pinewood Derby. In spite of your very busy life you know you must to carve out some time. If you decide to do so, I congratulate you for temporarily stepping away from an accelerated treadmill lifestyle to do it right.

We are all very busy. You feel it in the work place, when you talk to your friends, even when you talk to your kids.

---

1   On October 13, 2017, the Boy Scouts of America announced that under the Boy Scouts' new plan Cub Scout dens will be single-gender, either all boys or all-girls. The larger Cub Scout packs have the option to remain single gender or welcome both genders into a pack.

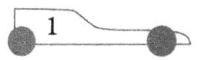

You can't miss it when you read the newspaper or watch the news. It seems every time we turn around there is some new high-tech device or app that can track, measure, and enhance every part of our lives, not to mention Uber, drones, Airbnb, TSA-Pre, solar panels, and electric self-driving cars. Technology changes the workplace, politics, healthcare, foreign policy, and even crime. Now we are no longer confronted by a masked man with a gun who wants to steal our money, but instead by an unseen computer geek from some remote location with a keyboard and a mouse who wants to steal your identity. Also, let's not forget how social media has changed how we interact and communicate with everyone, including our kids. Texting has not only become a habit, it's evolved into a tradition.

But I'm happy to say this state of acceleration has a solution – the pause button. When you press the pause button on a machine, it stops. But conversely when you press the pause button on humans we actually start up, but in a different way. We *pause* to reflect, to rethink our assumptions, to gather our values, to imagine what is fulfilling, rewarding, important, and truly necessary in life. Hitting the pause button helps us reimagine what is possible, and reminds us of the things we should not leave out of our lives. It helps us reconnect with our most deeply held values and beliefs. Ralph Waldo Emerson said it best: "In each pause I hear the call."

That's what's cool about human pause buttons. They allow you to mint a little time for yourself, to hear the *call* to be the parent you know you should (and want to) be. A Pinewood Derby experience gives you permission to slow down, spend time with your child, and provide memories that will linger in your child's and your heart forever. And when that happens, you will quite possibly connect some of the dots in your own life. If you give your child your Pinewood Derby best, I promise it will end up being a blessing rather than a bother.

As you approach your Pinewood Derby experience, it is helpful to understand what business you are in here. First, it's not as much about the car as it is about your son or daughter. I hope you will focus on the fact that it is your goal as a dad, mom, grandparent, neighbor or Cub Scout leader to turn on a light bulb in your child's head in a way that inspires him or her to see important values and aspirations anew. Or maybe you can stoke an emotion or feeling that prompts your child to act more intensely or differently about doing something together. It's about how, with your guidance, during each step of preparing your car, you help your children learn *beyond* building the car, which is why as their mentor you help your children in the first place. The car is just a means to a greater end. Though your aspirations may be to win, or to just design the coolest looking car, those goals run parallel to other great values you learn together along the way.

All over the country, schools, churches, community centers, and organizations value ways to cultivate character in our youth.

The Ultimate Pinewood Derby Experience

I might interject here, that Pinewood Derby cars back in the day were primarily known as a father-son activity. But as of 2017 the Boy Scouts of America has welcomed girls into both Boy Scout and Cub Scout troops, which broadens the horizons of young boys and girls on so many levels. Even so, girls have been participating in independently sponsored Pinewood Derby events for years. In fact, I saw a TV commercial recently that showed the progressive steps required to build Pinewood Derby cars. At first, the viewer sees close-ups of young hands, tools, and the cars coming together. At the end of the commercial the camera shot widens to show an excited group of young girls preparing to race their cars. Because the Cub Scout program is the prevalent Pinewood Derby game in town, even more girls will be exposed to this wonderful character-building event. And rightly so, because if Dana Patrick can drive a car in the Indy 500, daughters can easily also compete with each other or their big or little brothers in a Pinewood Derby, making it an even bigger family event than it was in the past.

The activities for our kids that work best are the ones that help the participants feel a sense of learning. Most of the time building character is not an individual accomplishment. It emerges from a sense of involvement with like-minded others who seek the joys and fruits of joining hearts, souls, and hands. Plus, it is a time you can surprise your son or daughter with a little extra parental love, leadership, and the generosity of your time. Especially if what you learn in this book also helps you build a car that has a very good chance of winning.

I hope you will commit to carving out enough time to do it right, because those young, "it's-fun-to-do-something-with-mom-and-dad" years fly by fast. Believe me I know. With three sons, now grown, our Pinewood Derby days are among the highlights of events relived and talked about at family gatherings.

So when Pinewood Derby time comes around, I hope you look forward to the chance to pause, step off your "treadmill," and experience something very old-fashioned and fun with your son or daughter. Your commitment to your child's next Pinewood Derby event is a path that will detour you slightly off your regular daily routine into an occurrence that is not only a learning experience for your child, but also personally restorative for you. As a father, or even a single mom, being your child's Pinewood Derby pit-crew chief, helps you reconnect with the things that are truly important in your life.

All it takes from you is commitment, a little of your time, four nails, four wheels, a block of wood, and being ready to enjoy, learn from, and teach your child important lessons from your Pinewood Derby experience.

It Takes a Village

Lesson One

To quote an African proverb, *It takes a village to raise a child*. I know, as a parent of five children, my wife and I could not have done it alone. If it weren't for others, any Pinewood Derby success as shared in this book wouldn't have happened. Everything I have ever learned about preparing and racing Pinewood Derby cars is the result of a "village." This event will also help teach your child that they are who they are because of other good people in their life. You, his or her Cub Scout leaders, the people who set up the track, those who conduct the race, and even those who bring the punch and cookies, are all important elements of any Pinewood Derby. Not to mention, those clever mentors who help any conscientious kid get his car to the end of the track.

Such cooperation, mutual respect, and sharing are all part of the Pinewood Derby culture. For example, I personally witnessed a group of dads help a grandfather (who helped his fatherless grandson) build a Pinewood Derby car. And even though the car turned out to be, as they say, *a real lemon*, several dads teamed up between heats during the actual derby to adjust this boy's car so it would actually roll to the end of the track.

How much better off the world would be if all villages felt the same way?

Even in what may seem as trivial as a Cub Scout Pinewood Derby, this village helped put a smile back on the face of a sad-eyed kid and his very frustrated grandfather. It was awesome to see other dads share their own little "faster-car" Pinewood Derby secrets to help a child and his grandfather tune their car and feel included. When I witness this kind of giving and helping, it reminds me of how important a cosmic perspective about life is. That is to say, with humility we realize what a tiny mote we each are here on earth circling the sun as part of this vast universe. A cosmic perspective is indeed humble, and as part of this earthly village it helps us see beyond our own circumstances, and that as an individual, I am not, as some people think, the center of the universe. After all we are all in this together, to not only help, but often to be helped.

These are great lessons that during a Pinewood Derby might just reinforce the Golden Rule even between apparent competitors. Which is an important lesson I wouldn't want lost on my own sons and grandsons.

The great thing about the many great people in organizations, especially Cub Scouting, that sponsor events like Pinewood Derbies, are the myriad of other experiences they desire to provide our youth as they grow – experiences that help young boys and now young girls to learn to negotiate the "race track" we call life. The average Pinewood Derby race lasts about three seconds plus or minus a tenth or two. At most Cub Scout Pinewood Derbies, if your car, on 42-foot track, runs less than three seconds, you will most likely win the race. Obviously winning is a fun part, but the important learning takes place before and after the race.

There's no doubt the Pinewood Derby experience teaches kids character, honor, and interpersonal skills that serve them well in life. And along with many other extracurricular activities available today (sports, music, arts) building and racing Pinewood Derby cars is also comparatively inexpensive. Plus, it allows boys and girls to spend time with something other than all the high-tech digital devices parents are reluctantly coerced into buying and sharing time with at the dinner table.

Even adults come away learning something and feeling good about Pinewood Derbies. I've been able to refine a few of these lessons and personal values myself by helping my own sons, grandsons and some of the neighbor boys without dads, build and race their derby cars.

As you read this little book, think about how you can help make your Pinewood Derby adventure worth every minute you spend in the "pit" helping your own child (or a child without a dad or significant adult) prepare for a Pinewood Derby race.

It Takes a Village

If you stop and think about it, what could be smaller and simpler than four plastic wheels, four shiny nails, a block of wood, and a child? Okay, the child may not be simple – just young. But we know that without practicing on "small mountains" boys and girls, will never reach great heights, and participating in a Pinewood Derby is a good place for an eight-year-old to begin preparing for the larger mountains of life. And as they say (whomever "they" is) "as the twig is bent so the tree inclines."

What I have learned about the physics of Pinewood Derby car construction (and there's a lot) is due to largely to experts who were part of my village. Fortunately, they were willing to teach me what they knew. But even so, my most important lesson is remembering that the experience is not about the car. It's about a son or daughter. The car is simply a means to an end, which reinforces closer relationships between children and their dad, and in some cases their moms.

The lessons I will discuss, even this chapter's lesson about the "village" concept, are truths, or actually *behaviors* you focus on, point out, and experience together, while helping any child prepare and experience a Pinewood Derby. I also hope a Pinewood Derby experience may become something during which some of your own values marinate, even as an adult, allowing some refining and growth of values you feel are important in your own life.

I am grateful for the things I have been reminded of during the Pinewood Derby experiences I have had with my own sons, grandsons, and some boys in our neighborhood whose cars I helped build, because there wasn't a dad to help.

I have also included Appendix A, in which I share ten steps that will help you build a faster Pinewood Derby car. This includes introducing you to my friend, and Pinewood Derby expert, Glenn Jewkes. More about Glenn later, but he is a great resource if you want to go the extra mile when building a Pinewood Derby car. I'm glad Glenn has been part of my Pinewood Derby village.

So let's get ready, set, and go create some synergy – the interaction of two or more agents or forces (sons and daughters with dads, moms, or any adult helper) whose combined effect is greater than the sum of its parts.

The Value of Tradition

Lesson Two

A friend of mine, a young father, shared a little of his life's story with me while we were on a bike ride early one morning. He told me about building a Pinewood Derby car with his dad when he was about nine and winning third place. That achievement qualified him to compete in the much larger district Pinewood Derby. He didn't place in the district race, but he received a large trophy for good sportsmanship, because even though he lost, he was so excited and happy for the other boys who won. In other words, as the great golfer, Jack Nicklaus once said, "To be a great winner, you must also know how to be a gracious loser."

The tradition of the Pinewood Derby is that lots of boys get to be winners *in many different ways*. Some are rewarded for design, theme, originality, speed, color, and being a good sport. Some leaders are wise enough to create other special awards that help a child feel better about his Pinewood Derby experience, though they need to be awards that are meaningful. I remember a boy who received an award for the best batman theme car in his Pinewood derby. It had little meaning because his car was the only Batman themed car in the race. He felt he received it just to fulfill the modern politically correct "everybody gets a trophy" requirement. I'm glad my friend's district had an award for sportsmanship, because it is an award that sends a real message about a real value to a young boy. You can imagine what it meant to him at age nine, because that's the story he pulled out of his Pinewood Derby memory bank thirty years later.

Participating in a Pinewood Derby is one of the great traditions all across America. Your little car is one in an event that in the past, over fifty million boys have enjoyed. As you build your car together, share a little history about Pinewood Derby with your Cub Scout, so that he or she feels they are part of a great tradition.

The Pinewood Derby tradition began with these words. "I wanted to devise a wholesome, constructive activity that fosters a closer father-son relationship and promotes craftsmanship and good sportsmanship through competition," spoken in 1953 by Don Murphy of Pack 280C in Manhattan Beach, California. And with that, the Pinewood Derby was born. Don's son was ten at the time, and the popular activity of that day was soapbox derbies. These cars were big enough that the boys actually rode in them. They were fairly complicated and expensive so many boys couldn't participate. "Dad" Murphy wanted to invent a similar activity to do with his son and the younger boys in his Cub Scout pack (a pack that numbered fifty-five boys, by the way), but one that didn't cost so much.

That's when he had the vision of racing miniature derby cars down a smooth, slanted track, using only gravity. Don had made model airplanes, cars, and boats, so he knew it could be done, and the idea of making and racing miniature cars immediately gained traction with the other pack leaders.

Don and several of the Cub Scout committee members, who were skilled with wood working and electricity, started with a two-lane thirty-one-foot track complete with a battery-powered finish gate made from doorbells and switches that lit up a red or white light bulb to indicate which car won. Today the whole finish line apparatus is computerized with feeds from the track to a lap top computer and a projector that displays race times to one one-thousandth of a second, indicating instantly which car placed where.

Murphy decided the car kit should consist of a 7 3/8" block of pinewood – thus the name, *Pinewood* Derby car. The little block of soft pinewood could easily be carved and shaped with no tool fancier than a pocketknife, and the axles were nothing more than little finishing nails. He and the other leaders assembled kits in brown paper bags, numbered them, and handed them out at the April 17, 1953, Cub Scout Pack meeting held at the Manhattan Beach Scout House. The boys had a month to turn the blocks of pinewood into cars.

On May 15, 1953, the Scout House at Manhattan Beach was filled to capacity with enthusiastic parents and Cub Scouts ready to race. When Don Murphy saw the looks of excitement on the faces of the young Scouts (and their fathers) he knew he had created something special. Don reflects, "I gave them [the BSA] my permission to proceed with the program. It was quite rewarding knowing I had made a contribution to the Boy Scouts of America and created a meaningful family event that has become a worldwide tradition among millions of Boy Scouts today."

The October 1954 issue of *Boys' Life* carried the first description of a Pinewood Derby; a one-page article describing Don Murphy's Pack 280C Pinewood Derby race. While the car specifications were drawn in engineering schematics and the illustrations included a derby kit, there was no mention of how to actually run a race or where leaders of local packs across the country could get car kits. The national Boy Scouts of America office hadn't found a supplier yet.

But in early 1955, the Boy Scouts found Henry Henning, who became their supply buyer. He asked Art Hasselbach, a model airplane builder, to create a kit from Don Murphy's Pinewood Derby design. Art created the car kit and boxed them in sets of eight to be sold to the Cub Scout Packs. *Boys' Life* first advertised these kits in June 1955 for $2.75.

In 1956, the Cub Scout Program Guide suggested scheduling the derby at the same time as the annual Cub Pack Blue and Gold banquet, which made it a winter event. But soon, it stood on its own as one of the premier Cub Scout pack activities.

The Value of Tradition

Most of the rules and regulations of the Pinewood Derby remain pretty much the same as Don Murphy wrote them over sixty years ago. However, you'd be surprised how creative dads have become in working within those simple rules to make cars go faster and faster. The car length was evened out at seven inches, but the other dimensions remained the same. In 1977 wooden struts projected from the sides of the car on which axles could be attached. In 1980, they gave way for the solid pine block with the axle slots on the bottom of the block of wood we see today.

The wheel design has also evolved. Originally they were just skinny wheels, but were changed to a wider tread in the late 1970s and have remained essentially the same since then with only minor modifications. When sponsoring organizations adopted the Cub Scout program, the tradition of the Pinewood Derby came along with it.

And what a great tradition it is.

I think God takes delight in our creations, even if it is something as small as a Pinewood Derby car. Just like my friend who as a boy received the sportsmanship award, we all live with the memories of our own creations and recognitions. For example, my now-grown son Gardiner brought out the Pinewood Derby car he and I built twenty-six years ago when we began preparing for his oldest son's first Pinewood Derby. Gardiner had kept the car we had built all that time. Now he wanted to use the same car body for his own son's first Pinewood Derby. Tradition!

The Ultimate Pinewood Derby Experience

When I saw our old car, I felt the value of the Pinewood Derby tradition, something we had participated in with thousands of other boys; boys who were now men participating with their own sons. It has added to his life, and will continue to add through the experiences he shares with his other sons.

Though some may feel we shouldn't do things in life a certain way, just because that's the way we've always done it, there are some things most enjoyed when they're done exactly as they've always been done. *That's* tradition.

The Importance of Creating a Goal

Lesson Three

When you open that little box with the nails, wheels, and block of wood to start on your car, you're faced with three Pinewood Derby options.

1. Are we going for speed?
2. Are we going for looks, unique design, or some kind of theme?
3. Are we going for both 1 and 2 above?

Your choice will flavor your effort and the time required to arrive at the finished product. Obviously, option three requires a little more time, planning, and effort, not to mention a bigger learning curve. One Pinewood Derby expert told me that if all the frictional factors associated with the rolling speed of the car were ideal because of axle and wheel alignment, wheel orientation, weight position, and lubrication, you could race the block of wood (almost) straight out of the box. All you'd have to do is somehow cut down or hollow out the block to make the five-ounce weight, and you could still win the speed competition.

This is essentially what we did with one of my grandson's cars. (More later.)

I'm an avid cyclist, and other cyclists frequently compliment me on my bike. It is a great bike: carbon fiber, aero frame, great wheels, and an awesome paint job. It really looks fast. In the bike world, you might say it's the equivalent of a Porsche sports car.

The other riders are mostly younger, thus faster. They are serious riders who also have really nice bikes. I'm seventy-seven, so just about everybody out there is faster than me. Enjoying their compliment, I thank them for noticing my ride and I respond, with: "I'm not very fast anymore, but at least I can enjoy *looking* fast."

Likewise, it's possible to make a Pinewood Derby car look fast, that isn't. But it's also possible to make a Pinewood Derby car that doesn't look fast, be faster. But if you don't want to worry about speed, and spend more time on a cool looking design, that's a lot of fun, as well.

This makes for a great discussion with a young child about how in real life so many people thrive just on appearances alone. It's like the Texas cattle rancher who has "lots of hats, but no cattle."

With the first car we built, my eldest son, Curtis, and I had to make a decision about cool design versus being fast. It was eye-candy or speed, but not both. We were in the process of selling my dental practice and preparing to rent out our home for our move to Kobe, Japan. Our household was in multi-task-overload. At that time our five children ranged in ages from six to fifteen, and my eldest son, Curtis, our ten-year-old, had his first Pinewood Derby just a month before our departure date. I wanted to make it a special event and do the best we could.

When he was eight and nine years old, our Cub Scout Pack didn't have a Pinewood Derby event. They did the space derby and the rain gutter regatta instead. So this would be his first and last Pinewood Derby before he would age-out of Cub Scouts. Unfortunately, there was no time to focus on both speed and creativity. But after a fun discussion, he decided he wanted to see how fast we could make his car.

I'll admit that neither of us has even one artsy bone in our bodies. Which is why we were so impressed by a really cool car entry that looked like box of McDonald's French fries with the fries sticking out the back of the car. It wasn't very fast, but it was the talk of the derby and that dad-son combo had just as much fun as if they had been the fastest and had taken first place.

Because we knew little about all the factors that make a Pinewood Derby car go fast, I relied on the local library. In my research I discovered a little ten-page Pinewood Derby booklet you could order for ten dollars. (This was not a trivial discovery, since there was no Internet or Google back then.) The instructions included in our Pinewood Derby car kit explained the rules, but not a lot on design. So with both resources in hand, we went to work. Speed became our goal, and once we decided on that aspect, we were able to focus on one thing without worrying about how it looked. We felt like the guy at the proverbial auto drag race starting line, who showed up in an old rusty clunker, but unknown to anybody, there was 550 *"Horses"* under the hood.

Enjoy the Learning

Lesson Four

Working together, using our little booklet, we cut the block in half with a gradual taper toward the front of the car and sanded it. It was thinner, but not nearly as thin as the cars we built years later. Curtis also wanted to name it. Because Japan was so much a part of our thinking at that time, he thought something Japanese would be fun.

We learned that there were two types of bullet trains in Japan. They both went the same speed, but one was a "slower" service, called the *Kodama* because it stopped at every city. The other was the *Hikari*, which means "flash" in Japanese. The Hikari trains stopped only at certain stations, so they were quicker to arrive at their final destinations. As best we could with a red magic marker, we inscribed the Japanese characters for *Hikari* on Curtis's car, and then put on a coat of clear, fast-drying varnish over the entire body. That was our design. Then we went to work on *Hikari's* wheels and axles, making them as efficient as possible. (We didn't want to see it making any stops along the way, like a *Kodama*.) Speed was our main goal. How we managed speed back then, compared to what we do now with my grandsons' cars is quite different, as you will see later in this book.

Our secret weapon (the little booklet I bought) said that it really helped if you put great effort in to polishing the axles to reduce friction between the axle and the internal surface of the wheel bore.

I had an ace in the hole when it came to polishing small things, thanks to my dental practice. My dental lathe could take a variety of different chucks to hold items to be polished while they spin. We could insert the little nails that serve as axles into one of the chucks. Then when they spun at a high speed, we could polish them with instruments such as emery paper, or compounds ranging from a coarse to fine grit that produced a high gloss finish. It was like polishing a gold crown! When we finished, you could have seen your reflection in those little nails – if they'd been bigger.

Our little booklet suggested putting a groove in the axles just inside the hub of the nail. That way when you inserted it into the plastic wheel bore the nail had less surface area in contact with the inside surface of the wheel bore. So we added a small groove in each axle with a file as it spun in my lathe. However, as I will explain later, I have learned since, that the groove also provided another entirely different benefit that contributes to increased speed.

Next, our little booklet said that if we lengthened the wheel base (the distance between the axles), the car would run straighter, with less tendency to zigzag, or bounce back and forth, hitting on and off the center or side rails of the track. After checking the rules to be sure we were in compliance, we used a little coping saw to cut a new slot on the bottom of the car to increase the length of the wheelbase. We then put the wheels onto the axles and pushed the axles into the narrow slots cut into the bottom of the car. Today, as I'll discuss later, we actually cut the slots off the bottom of the block and drilled our own axle holes into the sides of the block.

According to the rules back then the car had to weigh a maximum of five ounces. *Hikari* was just a shade light. We drilled some quarter-sized diameter holes in the bottom of the car centered between the two axles, guessing as to the best position for the weight. Then we added enough quarters to make the weight and put tape over the holes so the quarters wouldn't fall out.

It was fun determining how to accomplish each step leading to our goal of having the fastest car. I coached Curtis, but taught him how to use some of my dental equipment and supplies so he could do the work. He picked it up rapidly.

After we placed the axle and wheels on the car we needed to test it. So we lengthened our kitchen table by putting in all its leaves, raised one end a few inches and then rolled the car down the table, positioning the axles in their little grooves for the best alignment. At the time we wanted the car to roll straight and not veer to the left or right, which is not the case today. In Chapter Seven, I will explain why and how, years later, I learned to purposely have the car veer to the left to make it go faster (and why that works). More physics to learn!

Hikari was ready to go, with even a few days to spare.

Hikari was a lucky car (or maybe it was the dental-equipment) but it crossed the finish line first in all its heats. My son and I felt very satisfied with our teamwork. In his first and last Pinewood Derby experience, he won the fastest car award.

But even if he hadn't won, we had a great experience. We both learned a lot about concepts new to us: gravity, friction, momentum, and aerodynamics. But more importantly, we enjoyed an experience of working together for a common goal. I taught my son how to apply varnish, how polish an axle (using the tools at my office), how to hold the file while making grooves in the axles, and how to position the emery paper and polishing compounds. It renewed my awareness that we can always learn something new in striving to reach a goal. That's a great benefit of the Pinewood Derby experience. It requires setting and achieving a lot of little goals on the way to the big one.

I know now, that back then, we were not through learning about building Pinewood Derby cars. Over the years, with every car we built, we realized there were things we didn't know we didn't know. Years later we also learned just how much fun design and creativity, not necessarily going for speed, could be. For example, my brother built a car for our family reunion Pinewood Derby in 2010 that was an exact replica of a bottle of Heinz 57, in memory of our dad who loved Heinz 57 on his roast beef. Another brother built an exact replica of my dad's old Ute Liner motor home. They were really cool.

My eldest son has now graduated from college; successful in a career, and as an avid reader, enjoys learning. We are still sharing titles of books we have read and enjoyed. Was his desire to learn reinforced by leaning over a dental lathe, building a Pinewood Derby car and observing the results? Who knows for sure, but it was certainly part of the mix.

It is also true that together as a teacher and student we could enhance the enjoyment of learning. For example, my relationship with my eldest son reached a different level while (and after) we built our Pinewood Derby car together. Having become engaged in a common goal, our conversation became more than "How was school today?" We talked, discussed, and thought together. It was a synergistic experience. We had such a good time building that car, that I was a little sad when it was over. But it also made me look forward to building future Pinewood Derby cars with other sons, grandsons, and neighbor kids. After our first derby, I asked my son what he got out of the experience. He knew I wasn't just talking about friction.

He thoughtfully replied, "Learning was part of the fun."

He's right. Because a truly educated man never stops learning. (And then we were off to Japan.)

The Importance of Planning, Committing, and Working

Lesson Five

In Japan, our children attended the Canadian Academy in Kobe, an international school. It became their social network and activity environment. The Canadian Academy spanned first grade through twelfth and included kids from all over the world, brought to Kobe because of their parents' vocation or career.

We were happy to learn that the Canadian Academy sponsored an element of home – a Cub Scout pack! Eight or nine months after we arrived, we learned it was Pinewood Derby time. Gardiner, my second son, had turned eight the month we arrived in Japan and having watched us build his older brother's car he was excited to have his turn.

We sat down together and talked about our options. There were no dental office advantages this time. No Scout stores. We knew that it would take a plan and real commitment from both of us to rely on the resources available. We made that commitment, and then considered whether we wanted to go for best of show or go for speed. Like his older brother, he chose speed.

The Importance of Planning, Committing, and Working

Gardiner's brothers were both anxious to help. While we were in Japan this little band of brothers really got along great. Because of the distances from their friends, they spent most of this at-home time playing with each other. They thrived on each other's successes, and today, even as adults, they get along famously.

I telephoned my dad and asked him to mail me the "derby shoe box" stored in the basement of our rented-out home. In it was a tube of graphite, some extra wheels, axle nails, some polishing compounds, files, pliers, emery paper, and other odds and ends that we had accumulated while building Curtis's *Hikari* before we left for Japan. I also asked Dad to throw in a couple of extra Derby kits from the Scout store, some extra wheels and more axle nails. Although it took a few weeks to arrive (no Fed-Ex back then), we were ready to begin when the box arrived.

Instead of my dental lathe, we used a slightly slower, but still effective, 3/4" electric drill purchased at a Japanese hardware store. It worked just fine to spin, polish, flare, and groove the axles, and to shape and polish the plastic wheels. Once again we poured over the instructions, and found that crowning or rounding the running surface of the wheels was still the way to go.

But even so, there were a few changes we came up with this time to make the car even faster. For example, we filed not just one, but two grooves in each axle. This technique allowed for yet an even smaller surface area of the axle to be in contact with the inside of the axle bore while the wheel rolled. Bingo! Less wheel-to-axle friction would make for better speed.

But again, as it turns out, this was not necessarily true, as I mentioned earlier. I learned several years later another reason for those grooves. More to come on that.

Another change we made this time was to thin down the car even more than we did the first time. This made the car much more wedge like, and thus more aerodynamic. When it comes to most Pinewood Derby tracks (even though tracks are not that long in distance or time) aerodynamics still plays a role in the speed of the car. It may not be more than just a few hundredths of a second, but sometimes that can make the difference between winning or losing a heat in a race with other cars of similar speed and weight.

One of our Japanese friends who had never seen a Pinewood Derby race before suggested we use a Japanese fishing-line weight to help get our car up to five ounces. Sounds good, we thought. We followed Mr. Tsubokura around a fishing tackle store until he picked out a fishing weight shaped like a teardrop. It was weighted at the bottom, so that it flipped back upright each time you knocked it over. It reminded me of the Shmoos that had been popular in *L'il Abner* cartoons when I was a kid.

We drilled a hole in the cockpit area of the car and then dropped in the little weight. The top part was a little higher than the profile of the car, so it looked like the helmet of an

The Importance of Planning, Committing, and Working

Indianapolis 500 driver sticking up out of the car. We even painted on two dots for Shmoo's eyes. (This car is pictured on the cover of this book.)

Something I tried to teach my boys is that when you commit to something, it always seems as if a great gate swings open, allowing people, events, ideas, suggestions, and help to walk through. Such was the case with Mr. Tsubokura and his idea for adding the weight.

My son named his car "Made In Japan." Be sure and have your child name their car. That's part of the fun.

Somehow, whether by sheer luck or just because we worked hard trying different ideas (even though we didn't know what we didn't know) we actually ended up having the fastest car.

This time, however, the Cub Scout pack leaders added a longest rolling distance competition. Here is where our extreme efforts to polish and groove the axles, and use plenty of graphite, paid off.

After the customary race, each child rolled his car rolled down the starting ramp and onto the school basketball floor with judges recording distances rolled. Gardiner's car shot down the ramp onto the court, passed all the other markers, hit the wall at the end, and bounced back about three feet. It's no wonder he kept that car to this day. It was a double winner!

The beauty of a Pinewood Derby is the process it provides of making a commitment, making decisions, and then taking action. If you lose, it's not apocalyptic. It's not like losing a job, marrying the wrong person, choosing the wrong career, or making a bad investment.

Needless to say, the school's Pinewood Derby event was a little piece of home for my second son and his brothers. However, I sometimes feel bad that I never got to do a Pinewood Derby with my youngest son, McKay. The next two years in Japan the Cub Scout pack leaders opted for the space derby and the rain-gutter regatta. The following year when we were back home, he had aged out of Cub Scouts, and moved on to other interests. He became an accomplished photographer, learned to play golf, snowboard and play excellent basketball, which gave us ample opportunity to applaud his skills and spend time cheering him on.

Nevertheless, I hope the memories of his vicarious Pinewood Derby experience with his two older brothers energizes his excitement when his own two sons will become of age, eligible to participate in their own Pinewood Derby events in a couple of years.

Learning That Patience Is a Virtue

Lesson Six

After three years in Japan, we returned to Salt Lake City. I started up a new dental practice from scratch; my children grew, graduated from high school, graduated from college, got married, and began their own families. I went from age forty-three in Japan to age seventy-seven in Salt Lake with eleven grandchildren. Time passed as fast as my son Gardiner's Shmoo-driven Pinewood Derby car shot down the ramp at our Pinewood Derby in Japan.

Twenty-six years of Pinewood Derby dormancy had passed when my wife, Margaret and I decided to spice up a cold January winter with a visit-the-grandkids junket; first to Virginia to see Gardiner and his family, then to Ohio to spend time with our daughter Jen, her husband and their kids.

Gardiner is a practicing endodontist in Richmond, Virginia. At that time, they had four children – their eldest son, two twin boys, and a daughter as their youngest. (They've since added another set of twins, boy and a girl.) Our Ohio daughter and her military-career husband were stationed at

Wright Patterson Air Force Base at the time. My son-in-law is now a Major in the U.S. Army.

In Virginia (our first stop) the big news upon our arrival was that their eldest son Isaac was now a Cub Scout and he had a Pinewood Derby in about three weeks. Gardiner wanted to know, "did I want to help with their car while we were visiting?"

"Well, does your mother love chocolate?" I jumped at the chance.

When I asked my son if they had their kit yet, he said yes, but they also had a better idea. He went to a closet and brought out the Made in Japan Pinewood Derby car we constructed twenty-six years earlier in Kobe.

"We want to use the same car body you and I built in Japan," Gardiner explained. I was amazed he still had that car.

That weekend was full of teaching, thinking, planning, and strategizing. But now we have the Internet. We just googled "building Pinewood Derby car tips," hit the search key, and *wham*! Seventy-eight thousand results in 0.20 seconds!

We went to work. We had to hustle, since Margaret and I would be leaving in four days. We turned the kitchen table of their new home into a Pinewood Derby car design, assembly, and tune-up plant, the likes of which would give Toyota a run for its money.

Along with sorties back and forth to Home Depot, the UPS Store (using their scale to check the exact weight), and a hobby shop or two (for some decals), it all came together.

We did a complete makeover of the Schmoo car: new paint, "blue to red," new axles, and new wheels. We did everything to the car we had done years earlier. We took extra care with the axle polishing, grooving, and the alignment. We kept the weight over the rear axles. Schmoo even got a new helmet painted on his head.

This time, however, the rules did not allow crowning or rounding the running surface of the wheels, so we took extra care in preparing new axles and wheels, and really spent extra time aligning the axles so the car would run as straight as possible. We also experimented with something I'd heard about, which was raising the position of the left front axle so its wheel didn't even touch the track. This made it so the car actually rolled only on three wheels. Yes, this actually works.

My grandson, knowing this was his dad's first Pinewood Derby car body, suggested we use rub-on numbers to make a decal behind our Schmoo driver that read "1983-2010." He also applied a little rub-on Japanese flag.

Finally, we were finished, but so was the weekend. My wife and I headed for Ohio before the race happened. A couple of weeks later, my grandson's Cub Scout pack's Pinewood Derby event took place.

In today's world, some Cub Scout pack leaders don't always award first, second, and third place trophies, just certificates for design, aerodynamics, best gas mileage, and so forth. They did post times however. These leaders felt it was all about just participation without emphasizing the competition. Something that seems to be becoming more prevalent in these times of "political correctness." As they say, nowadays everybody gets a trophy, but more on that later.

Out daughter-law took videos of the races, which she emailed to us a couple of weeks later. I was proud of my grandson, because after each of the four heats his car raced in – all of which he won – I noticed in the video very subdued fist pumps as his car crossed the finish line first. I could see he wanted to be a good winner by not "spiking the ball," as it were. I could see how excited he was, but he worked hard not to make anybody else feel bad. It was as if he was afraid to scratch the urge to acknowledge victory for fear of what kind of celebration would leak out.

Yet what a wonderful "itch" it was. As Margaret and I watched this video, we delighted in our grandson being a gracious winner.

I have to admit, when I helped he and his dad do a makeover of my son's car, I sensed an important lesson for myself. It was patience, keeping the concentration on my grandson, and not on the car. Of course, both his dad and I could have done things better or faster than a nine-year-old, and of course, things went wrong from time to time. For example, some of the sanding wasn't just right; the axles needed more polishing, some of the paint wasn't evenly applied, an axle got nicked with the file making a groove, a plastic wheel broke, powdered graphite got all over his mom's tablecloth, and one or the other of us even dropped the car a couple of times.

Well, that's when my own dad's advice kicked in. At moments like these, he used to say, "Sometimes in life, you have to bite your tongue and swallow the blood." And smile. When you pinch a finger, or jab yourself with a nail tip, or spill some paint in the presence of your child, you must be careful what you say out loud as well as under your breath.

In short, any father will agree that any project with a nine-year-old will have moments that test your patience, your ability to not become bossy, and to take over for the sake of saving time, or gaining speed. Yes, patience is a virtue. My youngest son when he was learning to talk, for some reason always pronounced the word "virtue" as "Virgil." Our kids grew up, and we all chuckle about it now, thinking patience was a "Virgil" rather than a "virtue." My point, however, is that no matter what happens we must always speak in a calm patient voice to encourage, laugh, and keep the whole experience fun. We live in a world of very toxic language. Working side by side with my sons and grandsons, being aware of my own occasional tendency toward impatience (I'm better that way at being a grandfather than I was as a father, as my own sons and daughters can attest), I realized that I want to be an example of calm in the midst of chaos, that guy who can say to his own soul, "Peace, be still."

The Ultimate Pinewood Derby Experience

So a lesson we adults can learn from the Pinewood Derby is that you may need a couple of do-overs. Pinewood Derby cars and all its parts are like hotcakes. Sometimes the first try just "greases the grill" and you flip that first one into the trash. If that happens, with an axle or a wheel, just grin and go on to the next attempt, without offending God, your son or daughter by biting your tongue and swallowing the blood. Your child will learn patience from your example. Like my youngest son still reminds his siblings to this day, *patience is a "Virgil."*

Fun is More Fun if You Have Someone to Have It With

Lesson Seven

I love the spirit of the message on a T-shirt, my grandson has. Printed in a dictionary font and format it defines the word "Funner" (which is really not a word), but the text reads: *Funner, Noun, - Gooder than just fun.*

We will never lack for valuable and fun things to learn and do, because there is always more to learn and more fun to enjoy in life. But there's also something special about fun, be it a hobby, golf, fly fishing, skiing, cycling, hiking, cooking, or even building a Pinewood Derby car. I think any activity is more fun when you're not the only one doing it – when you are having fun with someone else, it is truly "funner" or "more gooder" than just fun.

For example, after the Pinewood Derby races are over, I've noticed that a crowd of dads always seem to gather around the dad whose kid had the fastest car, asking questions about how they carved it, where they placed the weight, and what they did to the axles.

I've always enjoyed sharing this information when asked, but after one derby in our area I heard a dad make this interesting comment in a grim voice, which made me wonder if he had had any fun. "Our car wasn't the fastest, but at least my son built his car all by himself."

I had mixed feelings about that comment. Did that dad feel bad because his son's car didn't win? Was he assuming that the winner's dad, had done all the work? Or did he mean that he hadn't helped his son at all?

I have always felt the overriding purpose of these Cub Scout Pinewood Derby events is to make it a fun family experience as much as you can, with lots of teamwork.

The Scout website (*www.scouting.org/CubScouts/Activities*) explains: "The Pinewood Derby is one of the most popular and successful *family* (italics added) activities in Cub Scouting. Pinewood Derby cars are small wooden models that Cub Scouts make with help from their families (including grandparents, or close family friends). Then they race the cars in competition. The cars are powered by gravity and run down a track."

I'm glad the website used the word "family." Some Cub Scouts may not have a dad around to help, but who's to say a single mom, or a neighbor, an older brother or sister can't help. Sometime other adults outside the family, such as a neighbor, friend, or an adult scout leader, need to pitch in. Or sometimes it's an uncle, or a grandfather, who can stand-in.

If the Cub Scout has a dad, however, I hope that no dad would just hand his kid the kit and wish him or her luck. It's important to work with your child; help, motivate, and teach him or her skills with primer, paint, sandpaper, varnish, and a tool or two. In short, to work as a team, with dad or mom as a "coach," especially in the values arena of a Pinewood Derby competition.

Adults, moms, dads, or an adult friend can be there to explain the physics behind some of the concepts that make the car faster. But it's a team effort with parents helping and guiding, not something the child has to tackle all by himself. The point isn't always to win, even though you may try your hardest to win (and winning is a really nice bonus). The focus is about learning and working together, enjoying the journey toward the goal together and being there to say, "Well, there's always next year," if this year turns out badly, or "That was sure fun, let's do it again next year."

I have a friend who takes his own Pinewood Derby track around the area with his two sons. They set it up and conduct Pinewood Derbies for groups in the Salt Lake Valley. He told me that he really understood how important it was to have fun when one little Cub Scout was asked to say an opening prayer at the beginning of a church-sponsored Pinewood Derby, and during his prayer he slipped in this plea: "Heavenly Father, please bless us tonight that if we lose we won't cry." Now that's a refreshing bit of honesty that teaches adults that children have feelings about the outcomes, so we need to be part of the team that helps them "paddle" along, to do the best they can.

The Ultimate Pinewood Derby Experience

Boys and girls will put a lot of effort into building and racing their Pinewood Derby cars with Dad, Mom, (or even a grandparent or neighbor). So if they feel like crying when they don't win isn't it nice to have someone around that loves them to help with a soft landing of a hard truth? There is a lot an adult role model can teach along the way as a simple Pinewood Derby car becomes a reality, win or lose.

When the topic of Pinewood Derbies came up recently at a Saturday afternoon family gathering, one of my nephews commented off-handedly to his dad, "We need to get hopping, Dad. Our Pinewood Derby is next Tuesday."

I thought with a pang about how many hours of collaboration and fun as a father he and his son had already missed. There are always a few cars on Derby night with the paint still tacky, and the steering not tuned. Sometimes it's a dead giveaway that Dad may have thought it was not important enough to get going early. However, I do know that sometimes life happens and late starts when preparing your car are unavoidable. Just do your best so your child doesn't feel that *Dad doesn't think I'm not important enough to start early.* You want to be careful NOT to send the message that projects notable to your child are not notable to you. So don't put off starting your Pinewood Derby project if you are inclined, as I am sometimes, to procrastinate.

Teamwork takes at least two. A dad can teach that principle by example. A lot of things in life require teamwork – especially in a future career or marriage. Don't send the impression to the younger half of your team that the older half thinks a last-minute lifestyle is okay.

I remember holding one of my son's hands in mine, tilting them at just the right angle while he held a little file, smoothing off the burrs on the little axle nails spinning in the drill. I remember laughing together after I showed him how to polish the running surface of his wheel using my dental lathe. (I, um, somehow forgot to tell him to hold something in front of the wet pumice rag wheel as it began to spin. There was quite a splatter effect.)

There can be a lot of parent-child, pre-Derby fun. And of course the Derby itself is a blast. But besides all that, after the race is over, while the dads, as I mentioned are chatting and networking, there is most always something else going on. While post-race dad-to-dad gathering of derby nuggets for next year's car happens, where are the kids? They're having fun.

They have moved past who won what. They hand their trophies, medals, or certificates to Mom, and then run up and down beside the track, shagging their cars and carrying them back to the starting ramp to race their cars against each other again and again; one-on-one, brother against brother, den against den, friend against friend. They find the fun in race after the race. No keeping score, no bragging. It's all about taking turns pushing the starting button to release their cars and watching them shoot down the ramp.

At one derby, during the competition, I watched as one Cub Scout's car started down the ramp, fishtailing back and forth. As the wheels bounced back and forth off the center guide rail, the jarring pulled one of the axles out of its groove. As we all watched in horror, that wheel came off. The car veered to the left, flipped over, bounced out of its lane, and rolled sideways across two lanes to the left, wiping out both cars in those lanes in the process.

When I say "horror" that's what *we dads* were thinking. The boy, however, was grinning from ear to ear. "Wow!" he exclaimed. "What a cool wipe-out!" It really was. A second later, we were all grinning. They tightened a couple of axles and ran that heat again. I was grateful for a race director who believed in following the spirit of the rules and not just the letter.

In the end, the ingenious race master awarded this boy a prize (I'm sure it was a last-minute inspiration) for causing the most awesome wipeout. After the actual derby, this boy with is car was just part of the crowd, running his car again and again. They had all moved on.

The nice thing about Pinewood Derbies is there are always worthwhile outcomes, win or lose. Life is full of sour and sorrow, but even in their midst, a bit of sweet is also present. Being the fastest car certainly isn't everything. That's why I applaud for other awards as long as they are about something true and meaningful to the child (more on this later). Every child deserves to receive some recognition and praise in life. Every child deserves to have a few bricks in their "great wall" of life that say they are winners, but in a way that rewards them for their actual courage in stepping up to the starting line.

It's even better, and the fun is "funner" if it was a team effort, from beginning to end, with a parent or another adult helper, who actually anticipated the experience as opposed to waiting until the deadline demands turn it into a typical last minute, *get-er-done* whirlwind.

You can't fake it without your child sensing your true enthusiasm and whether or not mom and dad are having fun.

If Something is Worth Doing, It's Worth Doing Well

Lesson Eight

I ended the previous chapter focusing on recognitions for awards other than first, second, or third place as the fastest cars. This chapter is about what I think is the best way to help a young child look at winning and losing. Although we have all heard the proverb that it matters not whether we win or lose, only how we play the game, I have to say that there's a little more to it than that. In today's competitive world, just playing the "game" rarely cuts it.

Be it youth sports or a spelling bee, kids seem to learn early that winning is very important in society – maybe not to God, but to people. I once tried to calculate per athlete, how much nations are willing to invest in their Olympic athletes, in both time and money, for the glory of a medal in our modern Olympic games. The rough estimate I came up with of the cost per athlete was staggering and showed me the value society places on winning.

It's a fact of life that sometimes we win and sometimes we lose. We all have an opinion about how important winning is. When it comes to Pinewood Derbies, should we encourage

If Something is Worth Doing, It's Worth Doing Well

our kids to participate with the intent to do our personal best *and win*, or just participate?

A Pinewood Derby is an early win-lose experience in a boy's life. It is a valuable opportunity to give a child information about his attitude and values toward winning and losing.

After our January trip that brought us to Virginia in time to help our grandson, Isaac, and his dad with their car, Margaret and I went on to Ohio, our next stop on our *visit-the-grandkids* junket. As I mentioned earlier, my daughter, her husband, and three more of our grandchildren were stationed at Wright Patterson Air Force Base. Talk about a coincidence! Another grandson, Mitchell, had just become a Cub Scout and his first Pinewood Derby was coming up in about eight weeks.

His dad mentioned that the Derby in their Cub Scout pack was pretty competitive, thanks to all the colonels, majors, and Ph.D. aerospace engineer dads in their Cub Scout pack. Did I mention at that time my son-in-law (now a Major) was then still a lieutenant?

I immediately understood that for this Cub Scout pack nobody was going to start off the evening with a speech about the Derby not being about winning or losing, but playing the game. No way! Yes, there would be awards for first, second, third, and fourth place. (Four lanes on the track.) I will say that even though the military rivalry was good-natured (it's part of the teasing and the fun) there was also a rather serious underlying competitive side to it about winning.

I'll admit to a few misgivings when it comes to youngsters about competitive activities that, by their very nature, create winners and losers. With competition in many things from little league baseball to Pinewood Derbies, you could join in just for the experience. But on the other hand, never awarding first, second, or third places, but instead only giving out participation certificates or prizes for show, design, and aerodynamics, doesn't let a child experience the reality that sometimes you win and sometimes you don't. Even in today's *certificate-only, politically correct, everybody-gets-a-trophy* trend, kids still see through those awards, knowing full-well who was fast and who was slow.

My question to you and only your answer counts. Are young souls too delicate for competition at that age? Does rushing them into win-lose competitive situations too soon leave them with bruises of losing that cause them to retreat instead of tackling the next challenge? Does it forever harm a young Cub Scout's psyche if he/she doesn't win first place at their Pinewood Derby?

I doubt it. Especially if the leaders see that every child has an adult, if not a dad or mom, to help them in the process of preparation, the race, and the outcome. I feel there is nothing wrong if as many kids as is appropriate receives some kind of recognition for their effort, but I think even the kids would vote for awarding the fastest cars as first, second, third, or

If Something is Worth Doing, It's Worth Doing Well

fourth place along with the other recognitions as part of the awards ceremony mix?

It is impossible to protect a child from the life-experience of winning and losing. It's pretty hard to avoid never experiencing the agony of defeat, even though we all want our youth to have the thrill of victory. If you want to win at anything, there is always the risk of losing.

My dad's philosophy was very responsible as he tried instilling my personal approach to winning and losing. He assigned me chores on Saturday mornings and gave me even more over summer vacation. My chores had to be done before I could spend time with my friends. Whether it was mowing the lawn, painting the fence, or cleaning the garage, he always used to say: "If something is worth doing, it's worth doing well." Even as a kid, I remember finishing the yard, and taking a minute to look at it, knowing that my dad would also be looking at it.

I still remember when I began looking at a freshly swept and hosed off garage floor, the edged and manicured lawn, or the smooth color of the painted fence, and having worked like a rented mule, feeling satisfaction of what I'd done. There was something internally rewarding about doing something well.

In any kind of competition, beyond winning or losing is always the satisfaction of having worked hard to do your best. Even though doing your best is not a guarantee of winning, nobody can ever take away that satisfaction. So why not do your best and try to win? Win or lose, no child deserves to go through life sitting on the sidelines barely visible as an un-special person. You may not ever win a Pinewood Derby, but to have a *goal* to be satisfied with just being an also-ran may affect a kid's future life accomplishments.

Never having done a Pinewood Derby as boy, I didn't learn what it was really like to lose until my baseball team coach moved me from second base to right field after I missed shagging a ground ball for what would have been an important out. Yes, he wanted me to "participate and play the game, but even at that age, every kid knows that it's the "klutzes" that get sent to right field because so few hits go there. I didn't like it, but I got over it. Baseball skills weren't part of my DNA. But in time, after my first swimming victory, and after my first victory in a mile-run, in sports where my heart was as important as physical talent, skill, and coordination, I knew the thrill of victory. I always remember those wins, but I learned that the upside of winning and the downside of losing were soon diluted, and forgotten respectively, by the approach of the next race or event. You had to do it all again. These victories and losses were not historic emotional events, but collectively they helped me experience the happiness of winning and the sadness of losing. Both experiences adrenalized my desire to work harder and set a goal do my best and hopefully get better. Believe me, I lost a lot more races than I won, and certainly no college rang me up or sent me letters of intent to sign with athletic scholarship offers. But I do know

If Something is Worth Doing, It's Worth Doing Well

the effort that went into the goal, win or lose, was more beneficial to my character than the occasional thrill of winning or the disappointment of losing.

As a result, I have come to feel that the best approach to any friendly competition, even in a Pinewood Derby, is to dive in with all your might and try your best to do it well. If winning isn't the outcome, there are still great rewards to be found in the journey.

That, I hope, is one take-away message of this book. One of the most important lessons of Pinewood Derby happiness is to try your very best. Try to win. I doubt any child who loses will grow up with any residual Pinewood Derby scar tissue. The shelf-life of the thrill of victory or the agony of defeat is less than a day. Knowing you tried your best, win or lose, lasts forever.

When my eldest son won his Pinewood Derby, it was as exciting for his brothers and sisters and his mom as it was for Curtis. They loved seeing him do well. The joy of winning is contagious; it spreads to brothers, sisters, families, whole towns, and cities. Life seems a little better when your team, your sister, little brother, son or daughter wins. But if you lose, that too will pass. And siblings and parents are there to point out the positive even while losing. It will be interesting under the new policies to see the outcomes of brothers competing against younger or older sisters.

I helped a friend who was working with his grandson to prepare their Pinewood Derby car. A whole week before the race, the car was ready to go, completely painted, its axles and wheels polished and graphited. He said that his grandson, slightly autistic but mainstream, spent a lot of time that week, just holding his car, looking at it, lying in the grass and admiring it, anticipating the evening of the race. They had done their best, and were ready to race, come what may.

Turns out they did win, which gave this boy a memory he will always cherish. In fact, he won the following two years as a Cub Scout. The other families in their Cub Scout Pack were glad to see him age out of Pinewood Derby competitions. When you give your all, it flavors the enjoyment in a way that always lingers longer than the actual victory itself. But for some kids winning a Pinewood Derby is especially wonderful. Especially if you're a runt like I was growing when it came to baseball, basketball, or football.

The desire to always do your best, even if it's a small event like a Pinewood Derby, can be a habit that provides much satisfaction. How can you maximize what's learned and the experience of experimenting with new ideas? For example, my grandson in Ohio had a lot of fun racing his custom-made aerodynamic Pinewood Derby car. But the next year when his Pinewood Derby came around again, he told his dad that he wanted to use the same ideas regarding the wheels, but this time he wanted his car to be the same shape as the Pinewood block as it came out of the kit, a rectangular shaped block of wood. They had to hollow out the inside of the block in the kit to get it down to five ounces, but externally it was the

If Something is Worth Doing, It's Worth Doing Well

same shape as it came out of the box. With a little help from Grandpa, we drilled the axle holes, placed the axles, followed suggested protocols, regarding weight placement, tuned the steering, and added graphite.

Then my grandson stained his new car a chocolate color, and glued a Hershey's candy bar label on its top. It was his "Hershey Chocolate Block" Pinewood Derby car. It was a perfect blend of non-aerodynamic shape and perfect axle alignment and weight placement. Once again, he won first place. It was the fastest block of "chocolate" in their Cub Scout pack.

Winning or losing a Pinewood Derby, though less dramatic by world standards can still be a great experience. Winning experiences are contagious, but you still have to keep all wins and losses in perspective and not burn down the town during a victory celebration or go into a week-long frump if you lose. The reason the Scouting program encourages these races is because of what our kids can learn and experience by preparing for the race, regardless of the outcome.

It comes back to making that commitment to build the very best car you can and see what you can learn by doing it.

Learning How to Determine What is Fact or "Friction"

Lesson Nine

To begin this chapter, a metaphorical play on words, I will begin by saying that there are three kinds of people. Those who know what they know, those who know what they don't know, and those who don't know what they don't know.

It is good to move from the first to the last.

Young or old, we all must learn what really matters in life – and that starts with discerning between what is fact and what is fiction when determining a course of action. In the Pinewood Derby world, however, it's the differences between fact and *friction*. Can a Pinewood Derby help teach that to a boy?

I think it can.

There are a lot of myths about building Pinewood Derby cars. One of these areas is about the importance of car weight. Much is done at races to insure no car is heavier than five ounces, as if an extra two or three tenths of an ounce beyond the traditional five-ounce rule makes that much difference. Many are quite articulate about the importance of weight, claiming that a few tenths of an ounce is critical. I

Learning How to Determine What is Fact or "Friction"

have observed that those people are more adept at language than science. Bottom line, Pinewood Derby tradition has promoted the idea that the weight of the car, like the amount of protein in your diet, is more critical than it actually is. True, it takes longer to stop a train than a car when the friction of braking is applied, but before the momentum of any extra weight enters into the speed equation, most Pinewood Derby races are over.

I participated recently in an adult-only Pinewood Derby. These races are usually called "outlaw" derbies, because anything goes. Also, my eldest son, Curtis, now an adult, entered two cars in one of these "outlaw" derbies at his work, and got second and third place. First place went to a car with a tiny built-in battery and fan. It literally shot down the track. Curtis said it was so much fun to watch that he didn't mind losing with his gravity-only cars.

The only rules in "outlaw" derbies are limitations on the width and length of the cars – just so they fit in the track lanes, but otherwise, it was wide open. You don't even have to use pinewood. You could use any kind of wheel or axle you want, bearings, bushings, razor wheels or whatever. You could also enter any car, including one your child used, one you built yourself, or one you borrowed from a friend or bought on E-bay. This was to encourage participation. Last of all, the weight limit was ten ounces, not the customary five ounces. The extra five ounces added to the fun and flavor.

The date was set, and the adult Pinewood Derby "throw-down" was on.

Although how your car looks is part of the fun, most derbies are won or lost because of the axles, the wheels, their alignment, aerodynamics, and lubrication. That was how my grandson, Mitchell's, Chocolate Block car won.

But as I said earlier, something greatly misunderstood in Pinewood Derby car racing is the issue of weight. There are a lot of theories about weight, axles, wheels, the best lubricants, the best wheel alignment, the best placement of the weight, the length of the wheelbase, and the aerodynamics of the car. They're important, but when it comes to weight, a heavier car does not necessarily override other, friction factors to which more attention and skill should be applied. There is even debate among some Pinewood Derby aficionados about a NASCAR-like side-draft as the cars run down the track next to each other.

But at the top of the mountain of misconception is the effect an extra ounce or tenth of an ounce of weight adds to the speed of the car, as evidenced by the traditional weigh-in and track length. In my opinion, weigh-ins are mostly a meaningless protocol. Yes, conformity to a five ounce standard does provide a level playing field. But checking to see that someone is not a tenth or two of an ounce over the five-ounce limit has very little – and most of the time nothing – to do with any differences in the actual outcome of a race. Extra tenths of an ounce of weight won't overcome the

Learning How to Determine What is Fact or "Friction"

downside of poor alignment, aerodynamics, weight placement, and proper lubrication.

A father I know felt very bad after their race because he felt his son's car weighed only 4.7 ounces (it lost) and the winning car weighed five ounces. At most Derbies, most of the cars will weigh five ounces or sometimes even a little less. But did his son's car really lose because of that one or two-tenths or even half ounce less weight?

Let's look at this issue this way. If all the cars where to weigh *exactly* the same, then why is the fastest car the fastest? It's mostly friction, weight position, aerodynamics, wheel alignment, and lubrication.

For a science project a young Cub Scout named John Cox built a little ramp about four or five feet long made out of angle iron shaped like a ski jump. That way he could roll little balls down the V-shaped ramp. Because each ball was the same size, they all had the same rolling friction. The only difference was their weight. Each one was made of a different material such as lead, plastic, wood, steel, rubber, and glass.

Down the little ski jump they rolled, shooting off the end into the air and landing on a piece of paper. John marked where each of the different balls landed. You would think the heavier balls would fly farther, because we think they gained more speed as they rolled, but they all went the same distance, no matter what they weighed, as long as they all rolled the same distance before flying off the end of the ramp.

The Ultimate Pinewood Derby Experience

On gravity-powered Pinewood Derby cars, if all friction and aerodynamic factors were equal, they would roll down the starting ramp or the track at the same speed as determined by Newton's thirty-two-feet-per-second law of gravity. A heavier car won't essentially "fall" faster than a lighter car. A brick of gold will not fall faster than a brick of wood. If all other factors were equal, even if one car weighs a little more than the others, they should all roll to the bottom of the incline in the same time – unless there are differences in friction, alignment, lubrication, aerodynamics, and weight placement. The car with the least frictional rolling resistance due to all these factors, and the least wind resistance will get to the bottom of the incline first, not the car that weighs more. The five-ounce limit isn't much of a factor until the bottom of the ramp is reached at which point momentum kicks in. An interesting point here about the importance of weight placement. The further back on the car the majority of the weight is centered, if only just the length of the car, the further it has to fall at thirty-two-feet-per-second^2. Thus, if all the other cars have equal friction and aerodynamics, a posterior weight concentration has a little further to fall and gain speed.

Once the cars are on the level part of the track, friction factors continue to affect the speed, but not along with momentum, which *is* related to weight. Again, we all know that it takes longer to stop a train than a car. If all the friction factors are equal, a heavier car will have the most momentum and slow down the least, and roll further. But since the Pinewood Derby cars are all within a fraction of weighing five ounces, the rolling friction due to wheel alignment, axle preparation, lubrication, and air resistance or aerodynamics, usually supersede any minimal differences in momentum factors, especially when the flat part of the track is only twenty or thirty feet long.

What seems to look like the winning car surging ahead is because the other cars slow down sooner due to greater friction or poor alignment and less aerodynamics.

If Pinewood Derbies were a distance competition, small weight differences would become more of a factor, but one or two tenths of an ounce is really not a factor for the length of most Pinewood Derby tracks.

In Japan, with Gardiner's car, weight mattered on the distance competition that let the cars go clear to the end of the basketball court (if they could).

In summary, weight position is important on the down ramp, and weight differences can be important on the flat part of the track. But minor weight differences aren't the major factor. Extra weight in most cases would not have changed the outcome of the race the father whose son lost was talking about.

In my "outlaw" derby, with the ten-ounce rule, I thought it would be a great arena to test speed versus weight. So I entered a five-ounce car with little miniature ball-bearing axles, razor-thin wheels, and very aerodynamic construction;

in other words, very low friction and very aerodynamic but still just five ounces.

Everyone arrived for the race. One ten-ounce car was a steel bar with axles soldered to the bottom, very thin and aerodynamic. There was the usual pre-race chatter about how "My car will be slow, because I just built it last night." There was also a little teasing by the younger dads about how slow old men, such as me, drive.

Of course, I came in for a lot of teasing with my just-five-ounce car. The common thinking was a five-ounce car wouldn't stand a chance against a ten-ounce car when it came to speed. But I just replied that I knew what I knew, and teased that maybe they didn't know what they didn't know. This was all good-natured rivalry, but I suspected there was even more underlying, unspoken competiveness among the men than you normally see among the kids at a Cub Scout Pinewood Derby.

As the heats progressed, my five-ounce ball-bearing car was so dominant over the ten-ounce cars that the race director confessed that there'd be no suspense during the final run-off of the four fastest cars. He asked if I would mind withdrawing my car from the finals?

With my *ball-bearing-axles-razor-three-wheeled-aerodynamic* car being cast out like a star into the firmament of Pinewood Derby galaxies, the race continued. (This car is pictured on the back of the book.)

Learning How to Determine What is Fact or "Friction"

Dads will spend hours helping their kids design and trick out the car with spoilers and fins. For sure, this is one of the fun parts of the competition. But time spent on reducing the friction factors is most important if you decide to go for speed. With the right alignment, wheel and axle preparation, even with great fins, and low aerodynamics, you can overcome the same speed issues at most local Cub Scout level races.

So it is in life's other arenas, it helps any child learn how to perform a little due diligence in things about life. It is important to learn the facts, ask critical questions, and seek expert advice if available. In the real world, quality preparation may save not only money, but also a lot of worry, wasted time, and unhappiness. That's something every child can learn by doing a Pinewood Derby.

Just because everybody thinks, says, or promises a specific outcome if you follow their line of thinking, doesn't make it true. We have all been duped and deceived because we didn't really stop and ask hard questions when buying a home, a car, or making an investment. And for young boys, when it comes to honesty, drugs, hard work, and education, it's important to stay your own course. Just because everybody is doing something, doesn't make it the right thing to do. And in the case of Pinewood Derby cars, adding extra weight for a faster car doesn't make it scientifically true.

Metaphorically, facing "friction" in life can be a blessing, because it is the "friction" factors in life that hold us back. If we can identify them and reduce them, we can do better – something I know that I know, and something a young child can learn, as well.

Pinewood Derbies are not major life-changing events, but even such a small experience can teach a child the value of looking with a discerning discovery eye. Though the positive values learned in one or two Pinewood Derbies may be like a single drop or two when it comes to raising the level of ocean, but in real life, over time, along with other experiences, those one or two "drops" add up.

And as a parent I was honored and excited to help a few boys raise the level of their ocean of values a tiny bit.

There are Two Kinds of Alignment

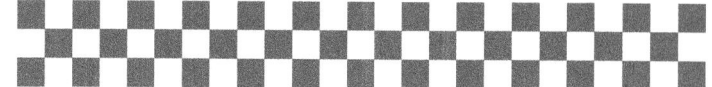

Lesson Ten

As I mentioned earlier, the block of wood that comes in the Pinewood Derby kit has two grooves on the bottom. You are supposed to put the wheels on each axle and push each nail tip snuggly into each groove. Even if just one wheel is placed in a position that would cause the car to veer slightly to the left or right a mere fraction of a degree, multiplied by four wheels, you have increased the car's rolling drag and friction. It's like four horses of a stagecoach not all pulling exactly the same direction. Perfect alignment is virtually impossible to achieve by just eyeballing those axles in the standard grooves on the bottom of the block. That's why drilling separate axle holes is so important.

But the other kind of "alignment" is an important principle in preparing a Pinewood Derby car. It is being aligned with and competing within the rules – simple honesty, a valuable lesson for every young man to learn, experience, and practice in life.

I grew up in little town called St. Anthony, Idaho. They used to let us out of school for two weeks in the fall to work in the potato fields picking spuds. We would go up and down the rows, filling up our wire baskets with potatoes. When they got full, working in pairs, one of us would hold open a burlap gunnysack while the other would dump the spuds in the sack. Two full wire baskets filled to the top comprised a full sack of potatoes. Up and down the rows we would go, placing each sack we filled in a line, but with every tenth sack we were instructed to set it out of line. This was so the potato boss could walk along the top or bottom of the field, and by counting the sacks that were out of alignment could know how many sacks were harvested and what our pay would be as well. (We were paid from ten to fifteen cents per sack, depending on which potato farmer you were working for.)

One of my friends, by not using two *full* wire baskets per sack and by putting an occasional ninth sack out of line, tried to fudge his numbers. Not only did he get caught, he also got fired and earned the reputation of not being trustworthy or honest.

These lessons applied in the potato fields were principles that also applied in our backyard sandbox, and on the neighborhood playground, my school classrooms, on the athletic fields, and in earning my Eagle Scout merit badges. Honesty is a foundational principle in life, and this value I learned growing up has served me well.

Pinewood Derbies offer a child a start in learning this important lesson in life. Even though a car that weighs a slight bit more than the others has no true advantage, isn't that why they have a weigh-in – to be sure no one cheats?

There are Two Kinds of Alignment

Today without any effort on the part of dad or child, you can buy really fast Pinewood Derby cars online to use in your Pinewood Derby event. Some may say that's not dishonest, but the objective of the whole Pinewood Derby event philosophy, is to build your own car together. Pinewood Derby expert, Glenn Jewkes (whom you'll formally meet in Appendix A) offers what he calls the Build-a-Car Experience. For a small fee, a dad can take his son or daughter to Mr. Jewkes and spend a couple of hours in his shop, walking though the steps of building a really fast car and using the tools and equipment needed. Mr. Jewkes does this because he knows not all dads have a workshop with everything necessary to build a great car. So as a mentor, he counsels a parent and child and lets them use his tools and knowledge, to build a Pinewood Derby car together.

In today's corporate world people make fortunes manipulating or shaping the truth. Many would have us believe that success and profit is not possible in today's business world without mischief and malfeasance. Cutting ethical corners has become a way of life for many. It has never been more acceptable than now to ignore traditional moral values in business and finance. Your word and a handshake have less and less value in today's world.

But financial ends never justify unethical means. Success is possible to those who possess skill, courage, integrity, decency, and generosity, and who do not misinterpret or cross ethical lines. Some may scoff and make fun of what they say is "old fashioned" thinking, but it is really nothing more than being true to the values kids could learn as kids participating in a Pinewood Derby?

These values are often faith-based, but they are also part of natural law and wisdom of the ages. I believe that we all have an inner moral compass, which intuitively helps us discern the difference between something that is right and something that is wrong. You just know when you are cheating that it's wrong; and you also *just know* when you are being cheated.

As I began to build our car with my grandson and his dad, who lives in Virginia, using our twenty-five-year-old "made in Japan" car, the rules now specified that we could no longer round off, or crown the running surface of the wheels. No problem. We just got some new wheels, and sanded away the injection mold seams and polished the running surface to a nice shine. We also polished the inside of the wheel bores with graphite. These steps were allowed by the rules.

We then read the rules about axles. They said nothing about forbidding grooves, so we grooved and then polished the axles.

The rules said that no starting devices were allowed. Isaac was puzzled. "What does that mean, Grandpa?" he asked.

I had heard that sometimes people would actually put little magnetized strips on the front of the car that held it in contact with the vertical starting pin at the top of the track. Then when the starting pin fell forward, releasing the cars to roll, the magnet would actually pull that car forward just a fraction of a second faster than the other cars.

There are Two Kinds of Alignment

"Isn't that cheating?" he asked. He knew the answer even as he asked the question.

Building the car to the allowed width, length, and weight is really no problem, but the rules allowed us to lengthen the wheelbase (the distance between the front and rear axles) on my son's old car. At the time we thought this technique reduced the back-and-forth wobble as the car rolled down the track. (Back then we hadn't learned the bent axle method yet. More on that to come.) There was no mention of the wheelbase in the rules so we left it as it was.

When we were working on my grandson Mitchell's car in Ohio, we had to be sure it was okay for axle placement to not use the grooves or slots already on the block of wood that came in the kit, but to drill our own axle holes. A simple phone call took care of that.

The most fun was the surprise when we phoned to ask if the rules specified how many wheels had to touch the ground. "What?" the person we called asked. "You want to not have all four wheels touch the track? Why?"

"Well," his dad explained, "if the total friction of four rolling wheels and axles equals *four*, what would the total friction be if one wheel wasn't even touching the track or spinning?"

Pause. "I see what you mean. Interesting! No problem."

It was the same with the bent axle; (again, the explanation to come) and though we couldn't round the running surface of the wheel, there was no problem because of how the rear axle holes were drilled into the sides of the car at a downward angle, those wheels once on the axle and placed on the car body were canted slightly so each wheel would roll only on its inside edge anyway.

My grandsons loved all of these techniques, knowing that we were obeying the rules, but thinking outside the box. As a result, they were excited to see their cars race.

My son asked one race director at a district-level Pinewood Derby about the left front wheel not touching the track.

Yes, that was okay.

"Then was it okay to not even put that wheel on the car and just use a little guide pin instead?"

There was pause. "I'll have to check on that." A few minutes later, he was back on the line. Nothing in the rules prohibits it. In fact, I think it's a cool idea."

That's the real fun of a Pinewood Derby. You have a set of rules, and the challenge is to figure out how to work within those rules by thinking creatively. How can you make your car faster by using those very rules?

I remember the revelation that occurred in Olympic high jumping at the Mexico Olympics several years ago because Dick Fosbury discovered, while he was still in high school, that he could jump higher by going over the bar with his back to the bar rather than facing it. He won a gold medal at the Mexico City Olympics and revolutionized the sport of high jumping with what is now called the "Fosbury Flop."

I recall a commercial used several years ago to increase the sales of a particular brand of pit-less dried prunes: "Today the pits. Tomorrow the wrinkles." That's the spirit of any

There are Two Kinds of Alignment

competition, always looking for ways to improve, go farther, faster, or higher, removing the "wrinkles," or building a better mousetrap as the old expression states.

Whatever the game, even Pinewood Derbies, part of the fun is being inventive and creative, as long as you work within the rules. We laughed and joked about building a hidden compartment for CO_2 cartridges that would be triggered for a jet-assisted start. Imagining such technology was fun. In fact, I showed Isaac a couple of YouTube videos that showed cars with these special adaptations allowed in "out-law" derbies for speed. But after that it was back to our car and our rules. It's just what you do. Every Pinewood Derby provides a chance to practice honesty and play creatively within the rules so not only are your car's axles aligned perfectly, so is your heart.

Even if someone else's car runs faster, you are still a winner if you don't cheat. Winners never cheat, and in a very important sense winners never lose. Such honesty in a Pinewood Derby may be a small step for any youngster, but a giant leap toward his future of personal integrity as an adult. I want my sons, grandsons and all the boys I've helped build cars feel how important that one lesson is. Because there is never a pleasant after-taste to a maliciously broken rule.

The Measure You Give Is the Measure You Get Back

Lesson Eleven

There is a verse of scripture in the New Testament (Luke 6:38) that reads: "Give, and it shall be given unto you. A good measure, pressed down, and shaken together, and running over will be poured into your lap. For with the measure you use, it will be measured to you,"

This always makes me think of grocery shopping for Cheerios and Fruit Loops when our children were small, and even now when we know the grandkids are coming to visit. After we arrive home inevitably one of the kids opens the new box of cereal, it always looks about one-third empty, "pressed down and shaken together." Because cereal is sold by weight not volume, it settles during shipping, leaving room at the top. I remember taking the almost empty previous box of Cheerios and pouring the remaining contents into the new box. I always imagined it was as if God were filling it back up to the top with extra cereal, "filled again to over-flowing." It's good to remember that much in life is sold by weight, not volume.

And what does this have to do with Pinewood Derbies? Looking back when I first helped Curtis, then Gardiner and Isaac, and also Mitchell with their Pinewood Derby cars, I realized how enjoyable these Pinewood Derby projects had been for me, and how much I had benefited by taking the time to really be involved with my sons and grandsons. It was so much fun to spend that time with them, their dads, and other boys I have helped, seeing how excited they were when their cars did so well.

To illustrate, once I attended a meeting of my local church youth leaders that sponsored our local Cub Scout pack, fresh off my Pinewood Derby experience with my grandson, Mitchell. During a discussion about our Cub Scout pack's forthcoming Pinewood Derby, I asked the group, "Do any of you know of any child in our pack who could use some help with his Pinewood Derby car?"

A few heads quickly turned my direction wondering why a seventy-plus-year-old would ask such a question. One man mentioned a Cub Scout named August, who entered a car the previous year, but didn't do very well. He expressed how disappointed August was during that derby, and how some of the other dads tried to help by making a few quick adjustments to his car between heats. In the subsequent heats, his car did a little better, but by the end of the Derby, he'd won the Best Gas Mileage Award, which traditionally goes to the slowest car. His single mom and grandfather had done the best they could, but he was still a pretty sad Cub Scout by the end of the evening.

It turned out I knew August's grandfather and he welcomed some outside help. So we went to work preparing for the upcoming derby. After the block was shaped with a band-saw, in August's terms, "like a skateboard," and we showed him how to drill the axle holes, August, who had some very definite ideas about how he wanted to paint his car, took over.

When he was all through, his grandfather let me know, and we arranged to meet at my dental office the next Saturday morning to work on the axles and plastic wheels. I showed August how we fastened the axle in the lathe. I let him help polish the axles and the running surfaces of the wheels. We got graphite all over our fingers as I showed him how to put the graphite onto the flattened toothpick and slip it into the wheel bore. After some jeweler's rouge and a little chamois wheel pressed against those spinning axles, we had them literally shining.

The next week I made an appointment for the three of us to visit Glenn Jewkes. Glenn is so into the Pinewood Derby culture on a national level that he has an official derby track in his basement. August tested his car (which he named Bullet) on this track so he could see it run before the actual race.

We let Bullet coast down Glenn's tuning board, and showed August how to rotate the bent axle so it would hug the rail, and also how to tap the powdered graphite in and around the axles. Then we ran the car for a few timed test runs. Wow! It was fast.

Knowing what most times were, having supervised many Pinewood Derby events in the area, Glenn confidently predicted to August that his car would win.

I gulped, not feeling as confident. But seeing the look on August's face, I sure hoped Glenn's prediction would turn out right, especially after August's disappointing experience the previous year.

The evening of the race, August was really excited. His car weighed in right at five ounces. His Grandpa Bob was going to help him refresh the graphite between heats, a step that the rules for this derby allowed. The computer randomly selected which cars would run in each heat. August's car was in the first heat. With three other cars all in position, on the four-track starting ramp, I could see how nervous August's mom was. The first time down the track would give a good indicator of how things would go for the rest of the evening.

Then they were off.

I was relieved to see the Bullet win its first heat by three car lengths. The smile on August's mom's face after living 2.9 seconds of forever was worth every minute we had spent helping August.

Because there was some kind of a computer glitch and the times of the first heat weren't recorded, they decided to rerun the first heat. This time the Bullet won by four lengths. I guess the graphite got warmed up. August and his mom were grinning from ear to ear and she was in iPhone camera heaven, shooting pictures to record the event.

As the race progressed, the Bullet raced in three more heats, winning all of them and posting the fastest times. When it came time for the four cars with fastest averages to go head to head, racing once in each lane, the Bullet won four more times. August won not only the first place trophy, but also the award for the most aerodynamic car.

A couple of days later, he and Grandpa Bob brought over a picture his mom had taken of August holding his trophy and the Bullet. I have the photo in my den, and as I think about it, I am glad he won, but I also remember another special moment during the whole experience.

Earlier that week August had brought his car to my house after he had painted it to show me the gold racing stripe. As we stood in the entrance, which opens onto our living room, August noticed our piano. After telling me how much he appreciated my help with his car, he asked if could pay me back by playing something for me on our piano. I nodded. He sat down and played a wonderful little tune he had memorized during his piano lessons. I thanked him and encouraged him to keep practicing, wishing I had followed my own advice when I was his age learning to play the piano.

(I conned my parents into letting me quit, because I thought I would become a future Olympic miler. Duh!)

As he left, I had this picture in my mind of a box of Cheerios, its contents having settled during shipment, then being opened and being filled again to overflowing. It's true; the measure you give is far exceeded by the measure you get back. He had won the trophy, but I think I had received a greater prize.

And do you want to know what the real pay-off was? During the adult "outlaw" derby I discussed earlier, when I was asked to withdraw my aerodynamic car from the final competition, the winning car that beat out all the other ten-ounce outlaw cars was August's car, Bullet. He had loaned his car to Grandpa Bob for the adult Derby. August was there, beaming from ear to ear as his grandfather won. He came over to me afterward, and said, "I know your car didn't race in the finals, but because you helped me and Grandpa build our car, you can share first place with us."

What a great kid! What a treasured experience.

As parents, single or otherwise, we all labor diligently to bring positive experiences to our children while trying to instill quality values. But there are times when a child such as August may need extra help. A sensitive neighbor, an uncle or even a grandpa like myself, can always ask, "Can I help anyone with their Pinewood Derby car?"

Whenever you put such service into action, it is never just about a car. It's about the child. As you help a child, he or she will in turn learn to help others. And you, as a parent, or granddad, will have your Cheerio box filled to overflowing. It is such a simple experience, one of taking a few common skills, helping a child build a simple little race car, and doing it in such a way that touches on values that lift him or her, and let you feel the satisfaction of service. There is something cool, win or not win, about experiencing this truth. I think the Bible said something about having done something unto one of God's children, it is the same as having done it unto Him.

It just feels good.

Learning to Feel and Express Gratitude

Lesson Twelve

A Pinewood Derby is one of many moments in life that contributes to the answer of the big question about what kind of grown person a child will become. Those four nails, four little wheels, and the block of wood, many times create an environment that reminds a young child how he or she can be above average, focused, committed, patient, happy, honest, humble, giving, and thankful. It doesn't matter that it's just a Pinewood Derby, but only whether the experience triggers the kinds of thoughts and feelings that will help a child learn character-building patterns in their own life, one of which is gratitude. As I mentioned earlier, "as the twig is bent so the tree inclines."

In our neighborhood lives a couple, two wonderful friends with whom Margaret and I share six wonderful grandchildren. Our son Gardiner married their eldest daughter. Our daughter-in-law's father shared with me a wonderful story about his eldest son, and my daughter-in-law's older brother, Steven, Jr., which I think illustrates the message of this chapter, and a value or character trait every child can learn because of a Pinewood Derby experience.

Steven, Jr., and his wife had been married just a year or so and were experiencing the joys of their first child when Steven, Jr., was diagnosed with a rare form of cancer. After multiple surgeries and rounds of chemotherapy, this awesome young husband and father, not yet thirty years old, passed away. The story is about when Steven, Jr. and his dad participated in their first Cub Scout Pinewood Derby. They worked hard on their car and won first place.

The next year Steve, Jr., was really excited about participating again in the Derby and had great expectations of winning again. So they built their second car, another terrific entry with drag pipes, a spoiler, and a great paint job. With enormous anticipation, they got into the family van to drive to the event.

During the drive, Steve, Jr., stood up in the van just behind the driver's seat (this was before the current seatbelt laws), leaned forward, and from behind, wrapped his arms around his dad's neck, gave him a big squeeze and said, "Dad, thanks so much for helping me with my Pinewood Derby car."

Arriving at the race, they stood in line for the mandatory (but as we discussed earlier not really beneficial) weigh-in. The lady who weighed in the cars took Steven's car, placed it on the scale, pointed to the read-out, and said rather abruptly

Learning to Feel and Express Gratitude

for a Cub Scout event, "Your car is disqualified. It weighs too much."

Steve, Sr., told me he stepped forward and said, "I'm sorry, but there must be some mistake. We weighed the car at home and it was right on five ounces."

Without an ounce of compassion, the lady put the car back on *her* scale, turned it so they could see where the needle hovered, and, as if she was trying to be cute, turned back to Steve, Jr., and said, "Read it and weep."

So off came the drag pipes and a couple of other parts to bring the weight down. They succeeded and the event proceeded. Wouldn't it be great if the story ended by them having won a second year, but this little book is *non-fiction*.

Steve, Sr., told me that in spite of the outcome of the actual race and the disappointing experience at the weigh-in, Steve, Jr.'s, hug in the van was the highlight of his evening. That big, heart-felt, thank-you hug on the way to their Pinewood Derby by far overshadowed the final outcome. Gratitude had filled a young boy's heart and bubbled up to bless his dad. Steve, Sr., said as a father, it made him feel he was doing a pretty good job.

It is said that successful journeys are sometimes characterized by time in the desert. In this case, I hope the "desert" moments in Steve, Sr.'s, life of missing his son who since passed away, will be characterized by a simple expression of gratitude in their van on the drive to their Pinewood Derby journey.

The Ultimate Pinewood Derby Experience

Looking back, of all the things I have enjoyed the most about helping out with a few Pinewood Derbies was seeing the expressions on the faces of those boys when they did well, and the satisfaction I felt for having helped. These experiences mean that I am relearning over and over a lesson I will never over-learn. It's this: I've had many opportunities in my faith and in my dental career over the years to offer service both as a clinician provider for my patients, and as a teacher or professor to many of my dental students. Some of these opportunities were much more visible than others. Some were not "seen of men," such as helping an elderly widow, snow-shoveling a neighbor's driveway, helping a young child learn to ski on a youth outing, and even helping a few boys build their Pinewood Derby cars.

While my family and I were living in Japan, I learned the expression: *Kage ga usui*. The literal translation means to "have a thin shadow." It refers to serving others quietly, without a lot of recognition, reward, or notoriety – serving with a *thin shadow*. That is the spirit of giving I want to refine continually, though I still have a way to go. One reward was August's little piano solo or, for Steve, Sr., that heartfelt hug from Steve, Jr.

As you help your own son or daughter, as you give of yourself, I am sure a little of that the joy rubs off on your child, in such a way that he or she may feel gratitude, and be more inclined to help others, even in their youth.

Learning to Feel and Express Gratitude

August gave me a glimpse into the boundless spirit of giving and gratitude that even boys can develop even before they are men. The year after I helped August and his grandfather with their car, the three of us worked together again on a new car. On the night of the race, August and his best friend, Jake, raced against each other in the first heat. Jake's car won, with August's car second. As the next three heats progressed, Jake won all three of his elimination races, and so did August. They both qualified for the final run-off as two of the four fastest four cars. In the first of the final heats, Jake's car won again. As the three final heats progressed, August's car won each of the last three, two of them by only two or three thousands of a second. In the end, August won the first-place trophy again, and Jake was second, with a total time difference of twenty-six thousands of a second difference between the two cars.

I hadn't been able to attend that nail-biting derby, but I talked to August's grandfather the next day. After hearing the story, I asked how August felt when he saw his car get second in the two heats that Jake won and realized that the competition was going to be close, and that he could possibly lose.

His grandfather said August was actually hoping Jake would win, because August had won the last year. Jake had placed third that year and the year before. Jake was August's friend, so August wanted Jake to win first place this year. That way, both of them could have first-place trophies and share the experience of having won first place.

What an example of the spirit of giving!

In the early twelfth century the rabbi Maimonides wrote that giving progresses through eight steps:

1. We give with our hands, but not with our hearts
2. We give with our hearts, but too little.
3. We give with our hearts, enough, but wait to be asked.
4. We give with our hearts, but want to put the gift in the receiver's hand ourselves.
5. We give joyously and enough, without being asked and do not need the pleasure of seeing the gift received.
6. We give and do not even want the receiver to know from whence the gift came.
7. We become willing to pool our gifts with others, not needing to know who received, or how the gift is administered.
8. The highest step is reserved to those who anticipate a need even before it occurs and give to prevent suffering or to help others help themselves.

One reason I wanted to write this book is because a Pinewood Derby may be that one simple event that sparks a thought or two in a young child about what he or she can do to move through these steps of giving. With such a focus,

Learning to Feel and Express Gratitude

children learn to feel joy in the success of others rather than jealousy when someone else wins.

Four nails, four wheels, and a block of wood have shown me new dimensions of the joy of serving others. My reward has been learning and relearning that there are ways to be creative, passionate, and to bring the wisdom of my age and experience to the happiness of someone younger. It was delightful to see the curiosity, imagination, and wonder as young minds like those of Curtis, Isaac, Mitchell, August, and even their dads, my own sons, and son-in-law, grasped a few concepts of what makes a little wooden, gravity propelled car, faster.

A man once said, we must always obey gravity, (as if we have a choice,) because it's the law. Serving others, may not be a law like gravity, but when we serve others we become the beneficiaries of something I think is a law. It's a law called "The measure you give is the measure you get back." The agency I have exercised to live by that law has allowed me to see the benefits of things that go beyond the wonders of gravitational astrophysics by something as simple as building a Pinewood Derby car. It has helped me discover and enjoy miracles, like a simple piano solo, or a son giving his dad a hug, or a boy who thrills when his car wipes out.

I hope that my sons and a neighbor or two didn't mind that this grandpa wanted to help, as my growing grandsons, like Isaac and Mitchell and Luke, along with Tayden, and

Wyatt, who three years straight, as twin brothers, took first or second in their Cub Scout pack Pinewood Derby.

Yet to come, are three other grandsons, Noah, Joshua, and Eli, who will experience the Pinewood Derby era in the near future.

But I also hope that part of the fun for all of them was, and will be, the feeling of being loved – sensing that their fathers and grandfather cared enough to pull out all the stops, put in the time to be with them, and build a great car *together*.

The Finish Line

Conclusion

I hope this little book has given you some ideas about making the most of your Pinewood Derby experience. (If you want to stick with it, I offer some practical tips in Appendix A to consider while helping your child build his next Pinewood Derby car.) Although it may sound a little preachy, I also want this book to complicate your life a bit, create a little stress, and maybe even just a tinge of guilt, the next time your Cub Scout son or daughter brings home that unmistakable box. At that time you will have to decide how much of yourself you're going to dedicate to this project.

There's nothing like the experience of helping your own son or daughter (or any child) build and race a Pinewood Derby car, even if you have to put forth a few dollars for some necessary parts, equipment, and tools to really do it right. It's a great investment, and you will most likely spend less than what you would normally speed to equip or outfit your son or daughter for most local youth sport leagues or drill teams. (Not to mention the registration fees and travel costs to various tournaments). Go for the gold, but at the same time, recognize that even the slowest car can lead to beautiful things in the life of a child – and in your own life.

That's the beauty of building a little Pinewood Derby car. It might be one of the rare occasions in today's world when you can actually build and do something with one of your children that doesn't have a screen, need a chip, batteries, and never needs to be re-charged. It will simply create fun and memories neither of you will ever forget, all because of a little time, dedication, four nails, four wheels, a block of wood, and of course – a little gravity. No charge for the gravity.

Winning Car Tips

Appendix A

Arriving back home in Salt Lake City, and with a month before Mitchell's Pinewood Derby, one of my receptionists in my dental practice asked if I knew a man by the name of Glenn Jewkes, of Jewkes Engineering. His web site is *www.jewekesengineering.com*. You can go there to see great pictures of axles, Pinewood Derby car wheels, car bodies he designed, and other aids to help you perfect your own cars. It's all available within the traditional Cub Scout Pinewood Derby Rules and Regulations. He was (and still is) a national Pinewood Derby expert who lives in the Salt Lake Valley.

I did not know him at the time but that didn't stop me from giving him a call, which led to discovering a new friend.

He willingly agreed to meet with me, and from the moment I set foot in his door, I entered a new realm of Pinewood Derby data. Glenn has forgotten more about building fast Pinewood Derby cars than I will ever learn. And he was willing to show me how to build a fast car using all the tips I have sprinkled throughout this book and in this appendix.

Glenn explained to me that the "Holy Grail" of Pinewood Derby success is aerodynamics, axle alignment, lubrication, and weight position. It is really beneficial he told me to drill new and separate holes for each axle rather than using the pre-cut slots on the bottom of the pinewood block in the kits. In other words, it's hard to achieve perfect axle alignment by pushing the axle nails into those existing slots."

As he took me into is shop to show me how he did it. He shared a lot of other tips, about the physics behind aerodynamics, his axle techniques, weight placement, and everything in between. They were things about Pinewood Derby cars I didn't know I didn't know. These tips made major differences in the performance of our Pinewood Derby cars and were tips I could easily implement and share with my own grandsons and their dads.

I'm very grateful that he was willing to let me share his knowledge and experience. The ten tips that follow, will help you build a faster car (if you take the time to implement them). You can push the limits to see just how fast you can really make a gravity propelled Pinewood Derby car go.

As I mentioned earlier, a man once said, *Obey Gravity – It's the law.* Here are ten ways to help you take the greatest advantage of gravity, by how you work with your gravity propelled package of four nails, four wheels and block of wood.

Winning Car Tip # 1
Shape Your Car Block

Imagine that ten Cub Scouts have climbed up a tree, each with their five-ounce Derby cars, and then dropped their cars all at the same time. The cars would accelerate as they fell at thirty-two-feet-per-second^2, because of gravity. The cars would all fall at the same rate and pretty much hit the ground at the same time. But if one of the cars was more aerodynamic and another car was thick and bulky, the more aerodynamic car (the wedge) would hit the ground first, even if only by fractions of a second.

In the extreme, if one Cub Scout happened to attach a little parachute to his car (so as to not let it smash when it hit the ground), that car would obviously land last.

The point is that shaping your car to make it aerodynamic is always effective and always creates a relative faster car. Aerodynamics, along with axle alignment and weight placement, is one of three major factors in determining the speed of your car.

Part of Pinewood Derby excitement is coming up with the originality and creativity of your car's design and shape. So have as much fun with your car's design as you want. After all, anything the mind can conceive you can design, and still have a relatively fast car. But if all other friction factors were equal the lowest, thinnest profile will encourage less air resistance and be faster.

If you want to have absolutely *the fastest* car, then you need to minimize the braking effect of the air as much as you can. Thus, your car should be as sleek and streamlined as possible. In other words, you want it to be shaped like a wedge, flat and thin, with a knife-edge front-end that slices through the air to minimize braking effects. I might add here, as you prepare your car body it's a good idea to leave enough thickness at the back to rout out a little rectangular box on the underside of the car that will hold a little tungsten weight block I will tell you about shortly. Additional weight will be needed to bring the slimmed-thinned down car up to the traditional five-ounce derby race weight. Also, while thinning your car body, start with the bottom of the block that has the axle slots. It will be necessary to eliminate those grooves anyway. At *www.jewkesengineering.com* you can see pictures of the little weight box or compartment and the tungsten weights that can be used in a thinned down aerodynamic car body.

Winning Car Tip #2
Prepare Your Wheels

Although it's not the case today, the Pinewood Derby rules used to allow you to round the running surface of the wheels.

But per the rules, we don't do that anymore, so here is what we do instead:

Winning Car Tips

1. Polish the internal surface of the axle holes using a good polishing compound and pipe cleaners that are the same size in diameter as the axle holes. Put the short end of pipe cleaner in the drill chuck, and while it spins slide the wheel on and off the little end of the pipe cleaner to polish the internal surface of the axle holes.

2. After the axle holes are polished you might repeat the same procedure, only this time use graphite on a section of pipe cleaner.

3. At every contact point where the wheel might touch the side of the car or where the axles would touch the outside of the wheel, burnish more graphite into the wood or the wheel by rubbing graphite into the axle hole surface area with a Q-tip.

4. On the outside side of the wheel where the axle hub contacts the wheel, polish or burnish with graphite the entire small inset area on the wheel. You can use the blunt end of a wooden Q-Tip as the wheel spins on your drill.

Wining Car Tip #3
Prepare Your Axle Holes

This is one of the most innovative steps of all. Thanks to Mr. Jewkes, I learned that this step is one of the most important key factors to a faster car. As I said earlier, it is best **not** to use the pre-drilled slots that come on the wood block for your axles. Instead, drill new holes on the sides of the car. Of course to do this, while shaping your car body, I mentioned in Car Tip 1 that it was necessary to cutoff the bottom of the block, eliminating those grooves. Once that is done you can drill new holes on the sides of the car body, front and rear.

Mr. Jewkes invented what he calls the "Block" to help align each hole in a perfect parallel manner with the other axle holes. First mark a dot on the sides of your car body where you want to drill your rear axle holes, left and right, on the sides, about 2-3 mm up from the bottom of the car.

But for the left front wheel that hole should be four to five millimeters up from the bottom of the car. That way, when all the axles are in place with the wheels on them, the wheel on the left front won't even touch the track. It is really quite simple! Now your car will run only on three wheels. You will need a #42, #43, or #44 size drill bit to make the holes. You can test the snugness of each size drill with each axle on a separate piece of wood with your axle nails before choosing which size drill to use on your car body. Sometimes the nail in the kit have varying diameters.

After you mark where you want to drill your axle holes, place your car on this special "Block" held in place with some small spring clamps. Next, place the block on its side (on the drill press platform) with the car body attached. Then place the little metal rod that comes with the block in the grove on the underside of the block. This tilts the block slightly so that when you drill the rear axle holes where you marked them, the drill actually goes into the wood at a slight downward (from horizontal) angle. Next, turn the block to the opposite side, and replace the little dowel rod in the groove and drill the opposite rear axle hole where marked. Using the little dowel with the block is only necessary for the two rear axle holes. You know you have done it right if when you place the rear axles in the holes with the wheels on them, the axles protrude out from the car at a slightly upward cant.

Next, drill the right and left front axle holes where you marked them with the block holding the car body flat on the drill press platform. Though they are both drilled horizontally, the left front hole will be a little higher on the side of the car body that the right front hole.

This is so the left front wheel when placed on its axle does not touch the track. The car will run faster if only three wheels touch the track, and the rear wheels touch only on the inside edge of each wheel (due to their axles being canted upward).

Winning Car Tip #4
Prepare Your Axles

If you look closely at those four little nails in the traditional BSA Pinewood Derby car kit, they have some rough edges and seams. In short they need to be polished. Therefore, you have to find a way of spinning them using a lathe, or even a hand-held ¾-inch drill. Place the nail in a drill chuck, use pre-cut sandpaper strips (starting with a coarse grit and working through four or five levels of grit) to polish the axle, using finer and finer sand paper as you go. After the sandpapers, you can switch to emery paper, or other kinds of pumice-like polishing compounds, bringing those axles to a fine, smooth, *frictionless* shine.

You may also put a groove in your axles using a small file as the axle spins. Just be aware that you might need some extra axles to practice on. And it is also good to place the grooves before polishing your axles. You'll also find pictures of these grooved axles on the *www.jewkesengineering.com* website. You can also save yourself a lot of time if wanted to buy your axles pre-grooved, polished, and ready to go.

The next thing in axle preparation is to flare the axle hub very slightly. This changes the ninety-degree angle where the hub of the nail meets the axle to more like ninety-five to one hundred degrees. That way the entire inside surface of the axle hub does not rub against the outside surface of the axle hole on the rotating wheel. This can also be done with a small triangle shaped file as the axle spins. Remember, you only need to put grooves and polish three of your axles. You virtually don't need to do anything to the axle that will go on the left front of the car. That wheel never touches the track.

Next, using a thin little rotating carborundum disc in a mandrel, drill, or on a Dremel, or carefully with one of the edges of triangular shaped file, cut a small, little slot on the top of the axle hub you plan to place on the right front of the car. The size of the slot should be such that you could place a small straight or slot screwdriver into it so you will be able to rotate that axle after you place it into its axle hole with the wheel on it in order to tune the steering. Be careful not to damage all your hard work and time spent polishing that axle.

Once the right front axle is all grooved, flared, and polished, put a wheel on it, and insert the axle into the right front axle hole. Leave about a standard credit card width between the side of the car and the wheel hub. With a little Sharpie Pen make a mark on that axle right where it comes out of the wood. Remove the axle and wheel from the car and with a file make a shallow notch at that spot so the axle is easier to bend at that point. Now, make a bend in that axle of about 5-10 degrees. On the polished side of the notch put something between the plier grips and the axle as you bend it so you don't ding up where you polished that axle. Of course you will need to do all the polishing the axle while it is still straight and then bend it last.

Winning Car Tip #5
Finishing your Car Body

At this point finish your car body using varnish, paint, stripes, decals, or even a new vinyl wrap, plus any little "doodads" your child may want to add. My grandson, doing an Army theme, wanted a Lieutenant Bar on his car because his dad was a lieutenant at the time. Just do your own thing to make it unique. The reason I suggest decorating your car now is because paint, varnish and doodads actually add a little weight, and later on, when you weigh your car, it is best to have it all painted or finished.

Winning Car Tip #6
Place the Weight in Your Car

If you recall when we talked about preparing the car body in Car Tip 1, I mentioned routing a little box in the bottom of the car in which to place the weight needed to bring the slimmed down car block up to the traditional five-ounce derby race weight.

I have found, again at the suggestion of Mr. Jewkes, that a small tungsten weight, which can be purchased on line (early planning necessary), works great. Place it in the little routed-out box directly under the rear wheels. Also, you may need to shorten the two rear axles if they protrude into the cut-out to enable the tungsten weight to fit into the box.

Also, if the box is longer than the actual size of the weight, you can add smaller tungsten cubes as needed to fine-tune the weight if it is still less than five ounces. Using this method is a very convenient way to adjust the weight of your car. This works best, because it puts the weight at the most desired location at the rear of the car. The farther back the better. The lighter the front of the car the better, because as the cars start down the ramp they are actually falling. The further back on the car the weight is, the further that weight is able to fall, even if only a few inches, creating more speed by the time the car reaches the flat portion of the track. This may save only a few hundredths of a second, but some finishes are that close.

Because once again, winning is about which car slows the least on the flat part of the track, if you hit the flat part of the track first, if your car has the least wheel friction, the best aerodynamics, the best wheel alignment, and steerage tuning, your car will slow down the slowest. This is the reason one car appears to be faster compared to the others. They all gradually slow down when they hit the flat track, as their momentum dies, but the winning car slows down the least.

Use aluminum tape (bought at Home Depot) on the bottom of the car to easily hold the tungsten weight block in place. You can even re-position it forward or back if you are able to test and time the car before the actual race.

It is important to position the tungsten weight as far back as possible for one other reason. As I will explain further in Car Tip 8, there is always a little wobble effect when cars roll down the track. This the result of the front or rear of the car bouncing back and forth, on or off the center guide rail that the car is straddling on the track as it rolls. So if the front of the car is as light as possible, there is less bumping friction to slow the car down, creating less friction or resistance that has to be overcome as the front wheels rub or bounce along the center guide of the track.

Winning Car Tip #7
Weigh and Assemble Your Car

At this point I suggest you get out a small kitchen food scale and weigh all the parts of the car together. This is done to meet the five-ounce rule of most Pinewood Derby race events. If you are over or below weight now is a good time to make adjustments. Sometimes it is necessary to drill out some of the wood, from the bottom of the car if necessary, if the single tungsten weight puts you over the five ounces.

Once you have everything at the correct weight, it is fun to assemble the car. Place the wheels on the axles, and insert the axles into the prepared holes on the sides of the car. With the rear axles, again, I suggest you insert the axles far enough into the side of the car so that there is about a standard credit-card thickness between the inside hub of the wheel and the side of the burnished graphited car body. It's the same with the right front axle and wheel. As for the left-front wheel (the one not touching the track), push it in far enough so it is tight against the side of the car and won't move or turn. Or you can even use a guide pin instead of an axle with a wheel, like I talked about with my grandson's derby car. When placing the right-front axle and wheel, place the axle the first time so the 5-10 degree bend points downward. More on this in the next Car Tip.

But for the moment, proudly hold up your assembled car and enjoy it together. Admire your effort. It's a job well done!

Winning Car Tip #8
Tune Your Car

Now that your car is all assembled, it is time to tune it.

What? How do you tune a Pinewood Derby car?

First get out your little tube of powdered graphite. (Be careful here, because that stuff gets all over everything.) Hold the car with one side of the car's wheels down so the wheels rests on the outside axle hubs. Then with the snout of the graphite tube, squirt graphite down each of the wheel bores on that side, front and rear (between the car body and wheel). It's a little awkward with not much space between the wheel bore and the side of the car. Spin those wheels a bit and add a little more graphite. The gaps on both sides of the wheels are a little narrow, but you can squirt and shake to get plenty of graphite down into the wheel bores.

Remember I mentioned earlier about a second purpose for the grooves on the axles? That second reason is because the cutout portion of the axles allows for more graphite inside the wheel bore between the wheel bore and the axle as the wheel spins. Some Derbys don't allow you to add graphite between heats. This little reservoir allows a little more graphite and may help maintain the maximum speed longer.

Next, do the same thing for the wheels on the other side of the car. Repeat this process, but this time from the outside of the wheels into the wheel bores between the axle hubs and the wheels for both sides of the car. Spin the wheels slightly. Remember, the left front wheel is not functional so no need to graphite that wheel.

Once everything is graphited you can tune the steering of your car using a large table or a long board that is at least two feet wide.

Put something under the table legs on one end of the table to raise one end of the table, then place your car on the higher end pointing straight down and let it roll at least eight feet. Be sure not to let it roll off the table or your tuning board.

As it rolls slowly, note if it veers right, left, or goes straight. The goal is to have your car veer to the left about ten to twelve inches by the time it travels eight feet.

With a little screwdriver, in the little slot you cut into the hub of that right front axle, rotate the right front axle clockwise or counter clockwise to adjust the steering. At first this will seem a little tricky because you don't have to rotate the axle very much to fine-tune it to veer left the desired amount.

Once this is done, you now have what Mr. Jewkes calls a "rail runner." This means as your car starts down the ramp at the Pinewood Derby, the right front wheel steers the car to the left so that it hugs and runs along the center rail for the length of the race, instead of bouncing on or off the center guide rail as it rolls.

Also because of the cant, the rear wheels are pushed outward to the hubs and stay there as they roll, rather than sliding back and forth laterally along their axles, without the inside hubs rubbing against the sides of the car. which slows the car. Also the canted rear wheels (where the weight is positioned) will hardly touch the center rail, leaving no lateral back and forth bounce on and of the center rail as the car rolls.

The shortest distance and thus the fastest time between two points is the straightest line possible. The less the wobble or bounce on and off the center rail, front and rear, the straighter the line, the shorter the distance and the faster the car actually travels from point A to point B.

Your car is now ready to race. Yea!

Winning Car Tip #9
Test Your Car On a Real Track If Possible

This may be a little more difficult and not always necessary, but if possible, you might check around and find someone who has a Pinewood Derby track and test your car on it. Google around in your area and I bet you can find one. When August's car was ready, as I mentioned earlier, I was able to test it on Mr. Jewkes' track. We were able to make steering adjustments and weight placement changes at that time by noting the fastest times.

Another option is that (rarely because if they let one they have to let all) if you get to the race early, sometimes the track is set up and they let kids do a few test runs before the derby begins. This may help you get some idea of how your car rolls. You can check the steering, and look for any wobble. (Don't forget to bring your tools to the track on race day, because you may be able to make minor adjustments between heats.)

Winning Car Tip #10
Race Your Car, Bring Home a Trophy

No matter what happens at your race, have fun. You are well-prepared and if you made the all-in effort to implement the steps, you will have a much greater chance of accomplishing your goal of having the fastest car, as well as (and more importantly) bonding over a rewarding father-son experience.

And when you're done, I hope you felt all the effort was well worth it.

About the Author

Dr. Barlow L. Packer began practicing dentistry in the Salt Lake City area in 1970. Prior to entering private practice he graduated from the University of Utah with a BA degree in psychology and a minor in Japanese. He then graduated from Northwestern University Dental School in 1968 after which he spent two years on active duty as a Captain in the U.S. Army Dental Corps during the Vietnam conflict. While engaged in his private dental practice, Dr. Packer spent hundreds of hours in post graduate continuing education and the study of diet and nutrition. He recently retired from private practice and is now an Associate Professor of Nutrition and an Attending Clinical Instructor at the University of Utah School of Dentistry.

Dr. Packer's second career (writing) focuses on a variety of simple, but important, aspects of everyday life. You can find other books he has written on *Amazon.com*. In addition to his love of teaching and writing, two of his favorite toys are a custom Seven carbon fiber road bike and a pair of Soul Seven downhill skis, which he still uses often, summer and winter. Dr. Packer believes that in life, the later years need not be inferior to the early years.

www.ingramcontent.com/pod-product-compliance
Lightning Source LLC
Chambersburg PA
CBHW071527080526
44588CB00011B/1582